Fascism vs. Capitalism

Fascism vs. Capitalism

LLEWELLYN H. ROCKWELL, JR.

MISESINSTITUTE

AUBURN, ALABAMA

Mises Institute
518 West Magnolia Avenue
Auburn, Alabama 36832
Mises.org

ISBN: 978-1-61016-624-9

*To the Patrons of this book,
and all who support the work
of the Mises Institute.*

Contents

Introduction

"Fascism" has become a term of general derision and rebuke. It is tossed casually in the direction of anything a critic happens to dislike. Even libertarians—themselves the epitome of anti-fascism—have been called fascists from time to time.

But fascism is a real concept, not a stick with which to beat opponents arbitrarily. The abuse of this important word undermines its true value as a term referring to a very real phenomenon, and one whose spirit lives on even now.

I describe the features of that system in chapters two and four, but for now we may say this. The state, for the fascist, is the instrument by which the people's common destiny is realized, and in which the potential for greatness is to be found. Individual rights, and the individual himself, are strictly subordinate to the state's great and glorious goals for the nation. In foreign affairs, the fascist attitude is reflected in a belligerent chauvinism, a contempt for other peoples, and a society-wide reverence for soldiers and the martial virtues.

The fascist takes his inspiration from the experience of war. During World War I, people from all over Italy, notwithstanding differences of region or dialect, found themselves joined together in a common enterprise. The war demonstrated what could be accomplished when people discarded their lesser allegiances and devoted themselves to the cause of the nation, which always means the national government.

Socialists tried to pretend that fascism was simply the most developed, if also decrepit, stage of capitalism. But the fascists made their opposition to capitalism perfectly clear. For the dueling systems of capitalism and communism they proposed to substitute a "third way." The means of production would remain nominally in private hands, but the state would play a substantial role in production and allocation decisions. The classical liberal devotion to individual rights would of course be spurned in favor of collectivism, but in place of the communists' appeal to the worldwide proletarian struggle, the fascists' collectivism would be directed toward the nation.

Is it really so unreasonable to note that these principles have not entirely died out? In the US, the public obediently pays homage to the military, readily absorbing the most preposterous stories about "keeping us safe" and protecting our freedom. The free market economy is spoken of with contempt, and enlightened state control and public-private partnerships of various kinds are proposed instead. "Public service"—which always means service to the state—is urged upon the young. John T. Flynn noted that one of the characteristics of fascism was the substantial role the military sector played in the economy. He could scarcely have imagined the case of the US government in the twenty-first century, when its military expenditures are nearly as great as those of the rest of the world put together.

The second part of this book honors those people whose lives and careers represent the very opposite of the fascist state. These are people who devoted themselves not to propaganda and plunder, but to truth and social harmony. These names—among them Ludwig von Mises, Henry Hazlitt, Murray Rothbard, Ron Paul—will be familiar to many readers of this book.

Each of these men worked against the grain. Hazlitt enjoyed considerable prominence, to be sure, writing for the *New York Times* (if you can believe it), and his book *Economics in One Lesson* has sold in the millions. But when he wrote *The Failure of the "New Economics,"* a systematic refutation of John Maynard Keynes's *General Theory*, he was nearly alone. Keynes had swept the boards, and the economics profession was in no mood to consider root-and-branch critiques.

And when we call to mind Murray Rothbard, Ron Paul, and Ludwig von Mises, we see men who likewise stuck to unpopular positions even though doing so meant far less prestige, fame, and influence than they deserved. The wonderful and unexpected result of their labors, however, is that the work of all of them is experiencing a renaissance among intelligent people. Murray's work is read and studied far more widely today than it was during his lifetime—precisely because so many people today are seeking out principled men who spoke the plain truth, whatever the consequences for themselves.

Mises collected no salary from New York University, where he spent his academic career in the United States. His was an unpaid position. He survived because a group of businessmen who appreciated the significance of his work paid him a salary. His colleagues, meanwhile, scarcely gave him the time of day—what use had they for a reactionary throwback to the nineteenth century?

Today, however, nobody remembers any member of the economics faculty of NYU from 1957. The undistinguished academics who shunned Mises have long since been forgotten, while the work of Mises himself is being studied more widely than ever. Mises has had the last laugh.

There is a parallel here with Ron Paul. Ron spent most of his public life in obscurity. The Republican Party treated him like an alien. The media usually did not understand him, and when they did, they found him too dangerous to expose to the public. He spoke to modest crowds, saying exactly the same things he says today.

No one is going to remember the people Ron opposed in his presidential runs of 2008 and 2012. No one's life was changed by Tommy Thompson, Duncan Hunter, Tim Pawlenty, Rick Santorum, Michele Bachmann, or any of the others. As Tom Woods points out, no one ever said, "My life was changed forever when I encountered the philosophy of Mitt Romney."

But Ron, the one the media and the political class treated with contempt, will not be forgotten. His books will be educating people for many years, long after we are gone. His courageous example will inspire as long as people respect truth-telling amid an avalanche of lies, and at considerable personal expense.

The parallel between these two men is not exact: Ron lived to see his own vindication, while Mises did not. Mises could scarcely have imagined the rising generation of bright scholars working in the Austrian tradition who would appear in the early twenty-first century. Ron watched as millions of people, most of them young, defied the finger-wagging of the anti-Ron establishment to cheer him, learn from him, and advance his message.

And this is one of the most encouraging aspects of the Ron Paul phenomenon: Ron's success is proof that the establishment media is losing the control it once exercised in American society. In the old days, three television networks and a handful of newspapers laid out the limits of what was permissible to discuss and believe. The corporate state, and its wars and bailouts, were portrayed the way the regime wanted. Today, the official purveyors of information are struggling to stay afloat. The *New York Times* and the *Washington Post* are seeing their revenues plummet. The network news, meanwhile, has been surpassed by the internet as a source of information for the public.

This is no time for pessimism, despite the great many problems we continue to face. Imagine if, in the midst of the Nixonian stagflation forty years ago, we had been told that within our lifetimes the following things would happen: (1) the Soviet Union would collapse, and with it the case for the planned economy; (2) the official opinion molders' monopoly would be decisively smashed; (3) interest in the Austrian School of economics would explode among American students; and (4) despite a media blackout, Ron Paul and his libertarian ideas would become a nationwide and even worldwide sensation that astonished the most seasoned veterans. We would have dismissed this as a fantasy.

That fantasy is today's reality, so why all the pessimism? Not to mention that we have the fiscal implosion of the US government to look forward to. That can only be a boon to the cause of liberty.

These are perilous times—for the state. Its hold over the public mind is slipping away. Its Keynesian tools aren't working to produce economic growth. The promises of the welfare state are certain to be broken. Public confidence in the state will continue to erode.

Again, this is no time for gloom. Perilous times for the state ought to be exciting times for friends of liberty. Our foe is the corporate state, described in detail in Part I of this book. Our strategy for victory is laid out by the great men chronicled in Part II.

The great struggle of liberty against power, which has been going on since time began, has reached a watershed moment. Let us not be mere spectators. With our pens, with our voices, with our contributions to our great cause, let us give history a push in the direction of freedom.

SECTION 1

The Reality
of American Fascism

CHAPTER 1

The Reality of
Red-State Fascism[*]

Year's end is the time for big thoughts, so here are mine. The most significant socio-political shift in our time has gone almost completely unremarked, and even unnoticed. It is the dramatic shift of the red-state bourgeoisie from leave-us-alone libertarianism, manifested in the Congressional elections of 1994, to almost totalitarian statist nationalism. Whereas the conservative middle class once cheered the circumscribing of the federal government, it now celebrates power and adores the central state, particularly its military wing.

This huge shift has not been noticed among mainstream punditry, and hence there have been few attempts to explain it—much less have libertarians thought much about what it implies. My own take is this: the Republican takeover of the presidency, combined with an unrelenting state of war, has supplied all the levers necessary to convert a burgeoning libertarian movement into a statist one.

The remaining ideological justification was left to, and accomplished by, Washington's kept think tanks, who have approved the turn at every crucial step. What this implies for libertarians is a crying need to draw a clear separation between what we believe and what conservatives believe. It also requires that we face the reality of the current threat forthrightly by extending more rhetorical tolerance leftward and less rightward.

---

[*]December 31, 2004

Let us start from 1994 and work forward. In a stunningly prescient memo, Murray N. Rothbard described the 1994 revolution against the Democrats as follows:

> a massive and unprecedented public repudiation of President Clinton, his person, his personnel, his ideologies and programs, and all of his works; plus a repudiation of Clinton's Democrat Party; and, most fundamentally, a rejection of the designs, current and proposed, of the Leviathan he heads. . . . What is being rejected is big government in general (its taxing, mandating, regulating, gun grabbing, and even its spending) and, in particular, its arrogant ambition to control the entire society from the political center. Voters and taxpayers are no longer persuaded of a supposed rationale for American-style central planning. . . . On the positive side, the public is vigorously and fervently affirming its desire to re-limit and de-centralize government; to increase individual and community liberty; to reduce taxes, mandates, and government intrusion; to return to the cultural and social mores of pre-1960s America, and perhaps much earlier than that.

This memo also cautioned against unrelieved optimism, because, Rothbard said, two errors rear their head in most every revolution. First, the reformers do not move fast enough; instead they often experience a crisis of faith and become overwhelmed by demands that they govern "responsibly" rather than tear down the established order. Second, the reformers leave too much in place that can be used by their successors to rebuild the state they worked so hard to dismantle. This permits gains to be reversed as soon as another party takes control.

Rothbard urged dramatic cuts in spending, taxing, and regulation, and not just in the domestic area but also in the military and in foreign policy. He saw that this was crucial to any small-government program. He also urged a dismantling of the federal judiciary on grounds that it represents a clear and present danger to American liberty. He urged the young radicals who were just elected to reject gimmicks like the balanced-budget amendment and the line-item veto, in favor of genuine change. None of this happened of course. In fact, the Republican leadership and pundit class began to warn against "kamikaze missions" and speak not of bringing liberty, but rather of governing better than others.

Foreshadowing what was to come, Rothbard pointed out: "Unfortunately, the conservative public is all too often taken in by mere rhetoric and fails to weigh the actual deeds of their political icons. So the danger is that Gingrich will succeed not only in betraying, but in conning the revolutionary public into thinking that they have already won and can shut up shop and go home." The only way to prevent this, he wrote, was to educate the public, businessmen, students, academics, journalists, and politicians about the true nature of what is going on, and about the vicious nature of the bi-partisan ruling elites.

The 1994 revolution failed of course, in part because the anti-government opposition was intimidated into silence by the Oklahoma City bombing of April 1995. The establishment somehow managed to pin the violent act of an ex-military man on the right-wing libertarianism of the American bourgeoisie. It was said by every important public official at that time that to be anti-government was to give aid and support to militias, secessionists, and other domestic terrorists. It was a classic intimidation campaign but, combined with a GOP leadership that never had any intention to change DC, it worked to shut down the opposition.

In the last years of the 1990s, the GOP-voting middle class refocused its anger away from government and leviathan and toward the person of Bill Clinton. It was said that he represented some kind of unique moral evil despoiling the White House. That ridiculous Monica scandal culminated in a pathetic and pretentious campaign to impeach Clinton. Impeaching presidents is a great idea, but impeaching them for fibbing about personal peccadilloes is probably the least justifiable ground. It's almost as if that entire campaign was designed to discredit the great institution of impeachment.

In any case, this event crystallized the partisanship of the bourgeoisie, driving home the message that the real problem was Clinton and not government; the immorality of the chief executive, not his power; the libertinism of the left-liberals and not their views toward government. The much heralded "leave us alone" coalition had been thoroughly transformed in a pure anti-Clinton movement. The right in this country began to define itself not as pro-freedom, as it had in 1994, but simply as anti-leftist, as it does today.

There are many good reasons to be anti-leftist, but let us revisit what Mises said in 1956 concerning the anti-socialists of his day. He pointed out that many of these people had a purely negative agenda, to crush the leftists and their bohemian ways and their intellectual pretension. He warned that this is not a program for freedom. It was a program of hatred that can only degenerate into statism.

> The moral corruption, the licentiousness and the intellectual sterility of a class of lewd would-be authors and artists is the ransom mankind must pay lest the creative pioneers be prevented from accomplishing their work. Freedom must be granted to all, even to base people, lest the few who can use it for the benefit of mankind be hindered. The license which the shabby characters of the quartier Latin enjoyed was one of the conditions that made possible the ascendance of a few great writers, painters and sculptors. The first thing a genius needs is to breathe free air.

He goes on to urge that anti-leftists work to educate themselves about economics, so that they can have a positive agenda to displace their purely negative one. A positive agenda of liberty is the only way we might have been spared the blizzard of government controls that were fastened on this country after Bush used the events of 9-11 to increase central planning, invade Afghanistan and Iraq, and otherwise bring a form of statism to America that makes Clinton look laissez-faire by comparison. The Bush administration has not only faced no resistance from the bourgeoisie. it has received cheers. And they are not only cheering Bush's reelection; they have embraced tyrannical control of society as a means toward accomplishing their anti-leftist ends.

After September 11, even those whose ostensible purpose in life is to advocate less government changed their minds. Even after it was clear that 9-11 would be used as the biggest pretense for the expansion of government since the stock market crash of 1929, the Cato Institute said that libertarianism had to change its entire focus: "Libertarians usually enter public debates to call for restrictions on government activity. In the wake of September 11, we have all been reminded of the real purpose of government: to protect our life, liberty, and property from violence. This would be a good time for the federal government to do its job with vigor and determination."

The vigor and determination of the Bush administration has brought about a profound cultural change, so that the very people who once proclaimed hatred of government now advocate its use against dissidents of all sorts, especially against those who would dare call for curbs in the totalitarian bureaucracy of the military, or suggest that Bush is something less than infallible in his foreign-policy decisions. The lesson here is that it is always a mistake to advocate government action, for there is no way you can fully anticipate how government will be used. Nor can you ever count on a slice of the population to be moral in its advocacy of the uses of the police power.

Editor & Publisher, for example, posted a small note the other day about a column written by Al Neuharth, the founder of *USA Today*, in which he mildly suggested that the troops be brought home from Iraq "sooner rather than later." The editor of E&P was just blown away by the letters that poured in, filled with venom and hate and calling for Neuharth to be tried and locked away as a traitor. The letters compared him with pro-Hitler journalists, and suggested that he was objectively pro-terrorist, choosing to support the Muslim jihad over the US military. Other letters called for Neuharth to get the death penalty for daring to take issue with the Christian leaders of this great Christian nation.

I'm actually not surprised at this. It has been building for some time. If you follow hate-filled sites such as Free Republic, you know that the populist right in this country has been advocating nuclear holocaust and mass bloodshed for more than a year now. The militarism and national-ism dwarfs anything I saw at any point during the Cold War. It celebrates the shedding of blood, and exhibits a maniacal love of the state. The new ideology of the red-state bourgeoisie seems to actually believe that the US is God marching on earth—not just godlike, but really serving as a proxy for God himself.

Along with this goes a kind of worship of the presidency, and a celebra-tion of all things public sector, including egregious law like the Patriot Act, egregious bureaucracies like the Department of Homeland Security, and egregious centrally imposed regimentation like the No Child Left Behind Act. It longs for the state to throw its weight behind institutions like the two-parent heterosexual family, the Christian charity, the homogeneous community of native-born patriots.

In 1994, the central state was seen by the bourgeoisie as the main threat to the family; in 2004 it is seen as the main tool for keeping the family together and ensuring its ascendancy. In 1994, the state was seen as the enemy of education; today, the same people view the state as the means of raising standards and purging education of its left-wing influences. In 1994, Christians widely saw that Leviathan was the main enemy of the faith; today, they see Leviathan as the tool by which they will guarantee that their faith will have an impact on the country and the world.

Paul Craig Roberts is right: "In the ranks of the new conservatives, however, I see and experience much hate. It comes to me in violently word-ed, ignorant and irrational emails from self-professed conservatives who literally worship George Bush. Even Christians have fallen into idolatry. There appears to be a large number of Americans who are prepared to kill anyone for George Bush." Again: "Like Brownshirts, the new conservatives take personally any criticism of their leader and his policies. To be a critic is to be an enemy."

In short, what we have alive in the US is an updated and Americanized fascism. Why fascist? Because it is not leftist in the sense of egalitarian or redistributionist. It has no real beef with business. It doesn't sympathize with the downtrodden, labor, or the poor. It is for all the core institutions of bourgeois life in America: family, faith, and flag. But it sees the state as the central organizing principle of society, views public institutions as the most essential means by which all these institutions are protected and advanced, and adores the head of state as a godlike figure who knows better than anyone else what the country and world needs, and has a special connection to the Creator that permits him to discern the best means to bring it about.

The American right today has managed to be solidly anti-leftist while adopting an ideology—even without knowing it or being entirely conscious of the change—that is also frighteningly anti-liberty. This reality turns out to be very difficult for libertarians to understand or accept. For a long time, we've tended to see the primary threat to liberty as coming from the left, from the socialists who sought to control the economy from the center. But we must also remember that the sweep of history shows that there are two main dangers to liberty, one that comes from the left and the other that comes from the right. Europe and Latin America have long faced the latter threat, but its reality is only now hitting us fully.

What is the most pressing and urgent threat to freedom that we face in our time? It is not from the left. If anything, the left has been solid on civil liberties and has been crucial in drawing attention to the lies and abuses of the Bush administration. No, today, the clear and present danger to freedom comes from the right side of the ideological spectrum, those people who are pleased to preserve most of free enterprise but favor top-down management of society, culture, family, and school, and seek to use a messianic and belligerent nationalism to impose their vision of politics on the world.

There is no need to advance the view that the enemy of my enemy is my friend. However, it is time to recognize that the left today does represent a counterweight to the right, just as it did in the 1950s when the right began to adopt anti-communist militarism as its credo. In a time when the term patriotism means supporting the nation's wars and statism, a libertarian patriotism has more in common with that advanced by *The Nation* magazine:

> The other company of patriots does not march to military time. It prefers the gentle strains of 'America the Beautiful' to the strident cadences of 'Hail to the Chief' and 'The Stars and Stripes Forever.' This patriotism is rooted in the love of one's own land and people, love too of the best ideals of one's own culture and tradition. This company of patriots finds no glory in puffing their country up by pulling others' down. This patriotism is profoundly municipal, even domestic. Its pleasures are quiet, its services steady and unpretentious. This patriotism too has deep roots and long continuity in our history.

Ten years ago, these were "right wing" sentiments; today the right regards them as treasonous. What should this teach us? It shows that those who saw the interests of liberty as being well served by the politicized proxies of free enterprise alone, family alone, Christianity alone, law and order alone, were profoundly mistaken. There is no proxy for liberty, no cause that serves as a viable substitute, and no movement by any name whose success can yield freedom in our time other than the movement of freedom itself. We need to embrace liberty and liberty only, and not be fooled by groups or parties or movements that only desire a temporary liberty to advance their pet interests.

As Rothbard said in 1965:

> The doctrine of liberty contains elements corresponding with both contemporary left and right. This means in no sense that we are middle-of-the-roaders, eclectically trying to combine, or step between, both poles; but rather that a consistent view of liberty includes concepts that have also become part of the rhetoric or program of right and of left. Hence a creative approach to liberty must transcend the confines of contemporary political shibboleths.

There has never in my lifetime been a more urgent need for the party of liberty to completely secede from conventional thought and established institutions, especially those associated with all aspects of government, and undertake radical intellectual action on behalf of a third way that rejects the socialism of the left and the fascism of the right.

Indeed, the current times can be seen as a training period for all true friends of liberty. We need to learn to recognize the many different guises in which tyranny appears. Power is protean because it must suppress that impulse toward liberty that exists in the hearts of all people. The impulse is there, tacitly waiting for the consciousness to dawn. When it does, power doesn't stand a chance.

CHAPTER 2

The Fascist Threat[*]

Everyone knows that the term fascist is a pejorative, often used to describe any political position a speaker doesn't like. There isn't anyone around who is willing to stand up and say, "'I'm a fascist; I think fascism is a great social and economic system."

But I submit that if they were honest, the vast majority of politicians, intellectuals, and political activists would have to say just that.

Fascism is the system of government that cartelizes the private sector, centrally plans the economy to subsidize producers, exalts the police state as the source of order, denies fundamental rights and liberties to individuals, and makes the executive state the unlimited master of society.

This describes mainstream politics in America today. And not just in America. It's true in Europe, too. It is so much part of the mainstream that it is hardly noticed any more.

It is true that fascism has no overarching theoretical apparatus. There is no grand theorist like Marx. That makes it no less real and distinct as a social, economic, and political system. Fascism also thrives as a distinct style of social and economic management. And it is as much or more of a threat to civilization than full-blown socialism.

---

[*]June 19, 2012

11

This is because its traits are so much a part of life—and have been for so long—that they are nearly invisible to us.

If fascism is invisible to us, it is truly the silent killer. It fastens a huge, violent, lumbering state on the free market that drains its capital and productivity like a deadly parasite on a host. This is why the fascist state has been called the vampire economy. It sucks the economic life out of a nation and brings about a slow death of a once-thriving economy.

Let me just provide a recent example.

THE DECLINE

The papers last week were filled with the first sets of data from the 2010 US Census. The headline story concerned the huge increase in the poverty rate. It is the largest increase in 20 years, and now up to 15 percent.

But most people hear this and dismiss it, probably for good reason. The poor in this country are not poor by any historical standard. They have cell phones, cable TV, cars, lots of food, and plenty of disposable income. What's more, there is no such thing as a fixed class called the poor. People come and go, depending on age and life circumstances. Plus, in American politics, when you hear kvetching about the poor, everyone knows what you're supposed to do: hand the government your wallet.

Buried in the report is another fact that has much more profound significance. It concerns median household income in real terms.

What the data have revealed is devastating. Since 1999, median household income has fallen 7.1 percent. Since 1989, median family income is largely flat. And since 1973 and the end of the gold standard, it has hardly risen at all. The great wealth-generating machine that was once America is failing.

No longer can one generation expect to live a better life than the previous one. The fascist economic model has killed what was once called the American dream. And the truth is, of course, even worse than the statistic reveals. You have to consider how many incomes exist within a single household to make up the total income. After World War II, the single-income family became the norm. Then the money was destroyed and American savings were wiped out and the capital base of the economy was devastated.

It was at this point that households began to struggle to stay above water. The year 1985 was the turning point. This was the year that it became more common than not for a household to have two incomes rather than one. Mothers entered the workforce to keep family income floating.

The intellectuals cheered this trend, as if it represented liberation, shouting hosannas that all women everywhere are now added to the tax rolls as valuable contributors to the state's coffers. The real cause is the rise of fiat money that depreciated the currency, robbed savings, and shoved people into the workforce as taxpayers.

This story is not told in the data alone. You have to look at the demographics to discover it.

This huge demographic shift essentially bought the American household another 20 years of seeming prosperity, though it is hard to call it that since there was no longer any choice about the matter. If you wanted to keep living the dream, the household could no longer get by on a single income.

But this huge shift was merely an escape hatch. It bought 20 years of slight increases before the income trend flattened again. Over the last decade we are back to falling. Today median family income is only slightly above where it was when Nixon wrecked the dollar, put on price and wage controls, created the EPA; and the whole apparatus of the parasitic welfare-warfare state came to be entrenched and made universal.

Yes, this is fascism, and we are paying the price. The dream is being destroyed.

The talk in Washington about reform, whether from Democrats or Republicans, is like a bad joke. They talk of small changes, small cuts, commissions they will establish, curbs they will make in ten years. It is all white noise. None of this will fix the problem. Not even close.

The problem is more fundamental. It is the quality of the money. It is the very existence of 10,000 regulatory agencies. It is the whole assumption that you have to pay the state for the privilege to work. It is the presumption that the government must manage every aspect of the capitalist economic order. In short, it is the total state that is the problem, and the suffering and decline will continue so long as the total state exists.

The Origins of Fascism

To be sure, the last time people worried about fascism was during the Second World War. We were said to be fighting this evil system abroad. The United States defeated fascist governments, but the philosophy of governance that fascism represents was not defeated. Very quickly following that war, another one began. This was the Cold War that pitted capitalism against communism. Socialism in this case was considered to be a soft form of communism, tolerable and even praiseworthy insofar as it was linked with democracy, which is the system that legalizes and legitimizes an ongoing pillaging of the population.

In the meantime, almost everyone has forgotten that there are many other colors of socialism, not all of them obviously left wing. Fascism is one of these colors.

There can be no question of its origins. It is tied up with the history of post–World War I Italian politics. In 1922, Benito Mussolini became the Italian Prime Minister and established fascism as his philosophy. Mussolini had been a member of the Italian Socialist Party.

All the biggest and most important players within the fascist movement came from the socialists. It was a threat to the socialists because it was the most appealing political vehicle for the real-world application of the socialist impulse. Socialists crossed over to join the fascists en masse.

This is also why Mussolini himself enjoyed such good press for more than ten years after his rule began. He was celebrated by the *New York Times* in article after article. He was heralded in scholarly collections as an exemplar of the type of leader we needed in the age of the planned society. Puff pieces on this blowhard were very common in US journalism all through the late 1920s and the mid-1930s.

Remember that in this same period, the American Left went through a huge shift. In the teens and 1920s, the American Left had a very praiseworthy anticorporatist impulse. The Left generally opposed war, the state-run penal system, alcohol prohibition, and all violations of civil liberties. It was no friend of capitalism, but neither was it a friend of the corporate state of the sort that FDR forged during the New Deal.

In 1933 and 1934, the American Left had to make a choice. Would they embrace the corporatism and regimentation of the New Deal or take a principled stand on their old liberal values? In other words, would they accept fascism as a halfway house to their socialist utopia? A gigantic battle ensued in this period, and there was a clear winner. The New Deal made an offer the Left could not refuse. And it was a small step to go from the embrace of the fascistic planned economy to the celebration of the warfare state that concluded the New Deal period.

This was merely a repeat of the same course of events in Italy a decade earlier. In Italy too, the Left realized that their anticapitalistic agenda could best be achieved within the framework of the authoritarian, planning state. Of course our friend John Maynard Keynes played a critical role in providing a pseudoscientific rationale for joining opposition to old-world laissez-faire to a new appreciation of the planned society. Recall that Keynes was not a socialist of the old school. As he himself said in his introduction to the Nazi edition of his *General Theory*, National Socialism was far more hospitable to his ideas than a market economy.

FLYNN TELLS THE TRUTH

The most definitive study on fascism written in these years was *As We Go Marching* by John T. Flynn. Flynn was a journalist and scholar of a liberal spirit who had written a number of best-selling books in the 1920s. He could probably be put in the progressive camp in the 1920s. It was the New Deal that changed him. His colleagues all followed FDR into fascism, while Flynn himself kept the old faith. That meant that he fought FDR every step of the way, and not only his domestic plans. Flynn was a leader of the America First movement that saw FDR's drive to war as nothing but an extension of the New Deal, which it certainly was.

But because Flynn was part of what Murray Rothbard later dubbed the Old Right—Flynn came to oppose both the welfare state and the warfare state—his name went down the Orwellian memory hole after the war, during the heyday of CIA conservatism.

As We Go Marching came out in 1944, just at the tail end of the war, and right in the midst of wartime economic controls the world over. It is a wonder that it ever got past the censors. It is a full-scale study of fascist theory and practice, and Flynn saw precisely where fascism ends: in militarism and war as the fulfillment of the stimulus-spending agenda. When you run out of everything else to spend money on, you can always depend on nationalist fervor to back more military spending.

In reviewing the history of the rise of fascism, Flynn wrote,

> One of the most baffling phenomena of fascism is the almost incredible collaboration between men of the extreme Right and the extreme Left in its creation. The explanation lies at this point. Both Right and Left joined in this urge for regulation. The motives, the arguments, and the forms of expression were different but all drove in the same direction. And this was that the economic system must be controlled in its essential functions and this control must be exercised by the producing groups.

Flynn writes that the Right and the Left disagreed on precisely who fits the bill as the producer group. The Left tends to celebrate laborers as producers. The Right tends to favor business owners as producers. The political compromise—and it still goes on today—was to cartelize both.

Government under fascism becomes the cartelization device for both the workers and the private owners of capital. Competition between workers and between businesses is regarded as wasteful and pointless; the political elites decide that the members of these groups need to get together and cooperate under government supervision to build a mighty nation.

The fascists have always been obsessed with the idea of national greatness. To them, this does not consist in a nation of people who are growing more prosperous, living ever better and longer lives. No, national greatness occurs when the state embarks on building huge monuments, undertaking nationwide transportation systems, carving Mount Rushmore or digging the Panama Canal.

In other words, national greatness is not the same thing as your greatness or your family's greatness or your company's or profession's greatness. On the contrary. You have to be taxed, your money's value has to be depreciated, your privacy invaded, and your well-being diminished in order to achieve it. In this view, the government has to make us great.

Tragically, such a program has a far greater chance of political success than old-fashioned socialism. Fascism doesn't nationalize private property as socialism does. That means that the economy doesn't collapse right away. Nor does fascism push to equalize incomes. There is no talk of the abolition of marriage or the nationalization of children.

Religion is not abolished but used as a tool of political manipulation. The fascist state was far more politically astute in this respect than communism. It wove together religion and statism into one package, encouraging a worship of God provided that the state operates as the intermediary.

Under fascism, society as we know it is left intact, though everything is lorded over by a mighty state apparatus. Whereas traditional socialist teaching fostered a globalist perspective, fascism was explicitly nationalist. It embraced and exalted the idea of the nation-state.

As for the bourgeoisie, fascism doesn't seek their expropriation. Instead, the middle class gets what it wants in the form of social insurance, medical benefits, and heavy doses of national pride.

It is for all these reasons that fascism takes on a right-wing cast. It doesn't attack fundamental bourgeois values. It draws on them to garner support for a democratically backed all-around national regimentation of economic control, censorship, cartelization, political intolerance, geographic expansion, executive control, the police state, and militarism.

For my part, I have no problem referring to the fascist program as a right-wing theory, even if it does fulfill aspects of the left-wing dream. The crucial matter here concerns its appeal to the public and to the demographic groups that are normally drawn to right-wing politics.

If you think about it, right-wing statism is of a different color, cast, and tone from left-wing statism. Each is designed to appeal to a different set of voters with different interests and values.

These divisions, however, are not strict, and we've already seen how a left-wing socialist program can adapt itself and become a right-wing fascist program with very little substantive change other than its marketing.

THE EIGHT MARKS OF FASCIST POLICY

John T. Flynn, like other members of the Old Right, was disgusted by the irony that what he saw, almost everyone else chose to ignore. In the fight against authoritarian regimes abroad, he noted, the United States had adopted those forms of government at home, complete with price controls, rationing, censorship, executive dictatorship, and even concentration camps for whole groups considered to be unreliable in their loyalties to the state.

After reviewing this long history, Flynn proceeds to sum up with a list of eight points he considers to be the main marks of the fascist state.

As I present them, I will also offer comments on the modern American central state.

POINT 1. THE GOVERNMENT IS TOTALITARIAN BECAUSE IT ACKNOWLEDGES NO RESTRAINT ON ITS POWERS.

This is a very telling mark. It suggests that the US political system can be described as totalitarian. This is a shocking remark that most people would reject. But they can reject this characterization only so long as they happen not to be directly ensnared in the state's web. If they become so, they will quickly discover that there are indeed no limits to what the state can do. This can happen boarding a flight, driving around in your hometown, or having your business run afoul of some government agency. In the end, you must obey or be caged like an animal or killed. In this way, no matter how much you may believe that you are free, all of us today are but one step away from Guantanamo.

As recently as the 1990s, I can recall that there were moments when Clinton seemed to suggest that there were some things that his administration could not do. Today I'm not so sure that I can recall any government official pleading the constraints of law or the constraints of reality to what can and cannot be done. No aspect of life is untouched by government intervention, and often it takes forms we do not readily see. All of healthcare is regulated, but so is every bit of our food, transportation, clothing, household products, and even private relationships.

Mussolini himself put his principle this way: "All within the State, nothing outside the State, nothing against the State." He also said: "The keystone of the Fascist doctrine is its conception of the State, of its essence, its functions, and its aims. For Fascism the State is absolute, individuals and groups relative."

I submit to you that this is the prevailing ideology in the United States today. This nation, conceived in liberty, has been kidnapped by the fascist state.

POINT 2. GOVERNMENT IS A DE FACTO DICTATORSHIP BASED ON THE LEADERSHIP PRINCIPLE.

I wouldn't say that we truly have a dictatorship of one man in this country, but we do have a form of dictatorship of one sector of government over the entire country. The executive branch has spread so dramatically over the last century that it has become a joke to speak of checks and balances. What the kids learn in civics class has nothing to do with reality.

The executive state is the state as we know it, all flowing from the White House down. The role of the courts is to enforce the will of the executive. The role of the legislature is to ratify the policy of the executive.

Further, this executive is not really about the person who seems to be in charge. The president is only the veneer, and the elections are only the tribal rituals we undergo to confer some legitimacy on the institution. In reality, the nation-state lives and thrives outside any "democratic mandate." Here we find the power to regulate all aspects of life and the wicked power to create the money necessary to fund this executive rule.

As for the leadership principle, there is no greater lie in American public life than the propaganda we hear every four years about how the new president/messiah is going to usher in the great dispensation of peace, equality, liberty, and global human happiness. The idea here is that the whole of society is really shaped and controlled by a single will—a point that requires a leap of faith so vast that you have to disregard everything you know about reality to believe it.

And yet people do. The hope for a messiah reached a fevered pitch with Obama's election. The civic religion was in full-scale worship mode— of the greatest human who ever lived or ever shall live. It was a despicable display.

Another lie that the American people believe is that presidential elections bring about regime change. This is sheer nonsense. The Obama state is the Bush state; the Bush state was the Clinton state; the Clinton state was the Bush state; the Bush state was the Reagan state. We can trace this back and back in time and see overlapping appointments, bureaucrats, technicians, diplomats, Fed officials, financial elites, and so on. Rotation in office occurs not because of elections but because of mortality.

POINT 3. GOVERNMENT ADMINISTERS A CAPITALIST SYSTEM WITH AN IMMENSE BUREAUCRACY.

The reality of bureaucratic administration has been with us at least since the New Deal, which was modeled on the planning bureaucracy that lived in World War I. The planned economy—whether in Mussolini's time or ours—requires bureaucracy. Bureaucracy is the heart, lungs, and veins of the planning state. And yet to regulate an economy as thoroughly as this one is today is to kill prosperity with a billion tiny cuts.

This doesn't necessarily mean economic contraction, at least not right away. But it definitely means killing off growth that would have otherwise occurred in a free market.

So where is our growth? Where is the peace dividend that was supposed to come after the end of the Cold War? Where are the fruits of the amazing gains in efficiency that technology has afforded? It has been eaten by the bureaucracy that manages our every move on this earth. The voracious and insatiable monster here is called the Federal Code that calls on thousands of agencies to exercise the police power to prevent us from living free lives.

It is as Bastiat said: the real cost of the state is the prosperity we do not see, the jobs that don't exist, the technologies to which we do not have access, the businesses that do not come into existence, and the bright future that is stolen from us. The state has looted us just as surely as a robber who enters our home at night and steals all that we love.

POINT 4. PRODUCERS ARE ORGANIZED INTO CARTELS IN THE WAY OF SYNDICALISM.

Syndicalist is not usually how we think of our current economic structure. But remember that syndicalism means economic control by the producers. Capitalism is different. It places by virtue of market structures all control in the hands of the consumers. The only question for syndicalists, then, is which producers are going to enjoy political privilege. It might be the workers, but it can also be the largest corporations.

In the case of the United States, in the last three years, we've seen giant banks, pharmaceutical firms, insurers, car companies, Wall Street banks and brokerage houses, and quasi-private mortgage companies enjoying vast privileges at our expense. They have all joined with the state in living a parasitical existence at our expense.

This is also an expression of the syndicalist idea, and it has cost the US economy untold trillions and sustained an economic depression by preventing the postboom adjustment that markets would otherwise dictate. The government has tightened its syndicalist grip in the name of stimulus.

POINT 5. ECONOMIC PLANNING IS BASED ON THE PRINCIPLE OF AUTARKY.

Autarky is the name given to the idea of economic self-sufficiency. Mostly this refers to the economic self-determination of the nation-state. The nation-state must be geographically huge in order to support rapid economic growth for a large and growing population.

This was and is the basis for fascist expansionism. Without expansion, the state dies. This is also the idea behind the strange combination of protectionist pressure today combined with militarism. It is driven in part by the need to control resources.

Look at the wars in Iraq, Afghanistan, and Libya. We would be supremely naive to believe that these wars were not motivated in part by the producer interests of the oil industry. It is true of the American empire generally, which supports dollar hegemony.

It is the reason for the planned North American Union.

The goal is national self-sufficiency rather than a world of peaceful trade. Consider, too, the protectionist impulses of the Republican ticket. There is not one single Republican, apart from Ron Paul, who authentically supports free trade in the classical definition.

From ancient Rome to modern-day America, imperialism is a form of statism that the bourgeoisie love. It is for this reason that Bush's post-9/11 push for the global empire has been sold as patriotism and love of country rather than for what it is: a looting of liberty and property to benefit the political elites.

POINT 6. GOVERNMENT SUSTAINS ECONOMIC LIFE THROUGH
SPENDING AND BORROWING.

This point requires no elaboration because it is no longer hidden. There was stimulus 1 and stimulus 2, both of which are so discredited that stimulus 3 will have to adopt a new name. Let's call it the American Jobs Act.

With a prime-time speech, Obama argued in favor of this program with some of the most asinine economic analysis I've ever heard. He mused about how is it that people are unemployed at a time when schools, bridges, and infrastructure need repairing. He ordered that supply and demand come together to match up needed work with jobs.

Hello? The schools, bridges, and infrastructure that Obama refers to are all built and maintained by the state. That's why they are falling apart. And the reason that people don't have jobs is because the state has made it too expensive to hire them. It's not complicated. To sit around and dream of other scenarios is no different from wishing that water flowed uphill or that rocks would float in the air. It amounts to a denial of reality.

Still, Obama went on, invoking the old fascistic longing for national greatness. "Building a world-class transportation system," he said, "is part of what made us an economic superpower." Then he asked, "We're going to sit back and watch China build newer airports and faster railroads?"

Well, the answer to that question is yes. And you know what? It doesn't hurt a single American for a person in China to travel on a faster railroad than we do. To claim otherwise is an incitement to nationalist hysteria.

As for the rest of this program, Obama promised yet another long list of spending projects. Let's just mention the reality: No government in the history of the world has spent as much, borrowed as much, and created as much fake money as the United States. If the United States doesn't qualify as a fascist state in this sense, no government ever has.

None of this would be possible but for the role of the Federal Reserve, the great lender to the world. This institution is absolutely critical to US fiscal policy. There is no way that the national debt could increase at a rate of $4 billion per day without this institution.

Under a gold standard, all of this maniacal spending would come to an end. And if US debt were priced on the market with a default premium, we would be looking at a rating far less than A+.

Point 7. Militarism is a mainstay of government spending.

Have you ever noticed that the military budget is never seriously discussed in policy debates? The United States spends more than most of the rest of the world combined.

And yet to hear our leaders talk, the United States is just a tiny commercial republic that wants peace but is constantly under threat from the world. They would have us believe that we all stand naked and vulnerable. The whole thing is a ghastly lie. The United States is a global military empire and the main threat to peace around the world today.

To visualize US military spending as compared with other countries is truly shocking. One bar chart you can easily look up shows the US trillion-dollar-plus military budget as a skyscraper surrounded by tiny huts. As for the next highest spender, China spends 1/10th as much as the United States.

Where is the debate about this policy? Where is the discussion? It is not going on. It is just assumed by both parties that it is essential for the US way of life that the United States be the most deadly country on the planet, threatening everyone with nuclear extinction unless they obey. This should be considered a fiscal and moral outrage by every civilized person.

This isn't only about the armed services, the military contractors, the CIA death squads. It is also about how police at all levels have taken on military-like postures. This goes for the local police, state police, and even the crossing guards in our communities. The commissar mentality, the trigger-happy thuggishness, has become the norm throughout the whole of society.

If you want to witness outrages, it is not hard. Try coming into this country from Canada or Mexico. See the bullet-proof-vest-wearing, heavily armed, jackbooted thugs running dogs up and down car lanes, searching people randomly, harassing innocents, asking rude and intrusive questions.

You get the strong impression that you are entering a police state. That impression would be correct.

Yet for the man on the street, the answer to all social problems seems to be more jails, longer terms, more enforcement, more arbitrary power, more crackdowns, more capital punishments, more authority. Where does all of this end? And will the end come before we realize what has happened to our once-free country?

POINT 8. MILITARY SPENDING HAS IMPERIALIST AIMS.

Ronald Reagan used to claim that his military buildup was essential to keeping the peace. The history of US foreign policy just since the 1980s has shown that this is wrong. We've had one war after another, wars waged by the United States against noncompliant countries, and the creation of even more client states and colonies.

US military strength has led not to peace but the opposite. It has caused most people in the world to regard the United States as a threat, and it has led to unconscionable wars on many countries. Wars of aggression were defined at Nuremberg as crimes against humanity.

Obama was supposed to end this. He never promised to do so, but his supporters all believed that he would. Instead, he has done the opposite. He has increased troop levels, entrenched wars, and started new ones. In reality, he has presided over a warfare state just as vicious as any in history. The difference this time is that the Left is no longer criticizing the US role in the world. In that sense, Obama is the best thing ever to happen to the warmongers and the military-industrial complex.

As for the Right in this country, it once opposed this kind of military fascism. But all that changed after the beginning of the Cold War. The Right was led into a terrible ideological shift, well documented in Murray Rothbard's neglected masterpiece *The Betrayal of the American Right*. In the name of stopping communism, the right came to follow ex–CIA agent Bill Buckley's endorsement of a totalitarian bureaucracy at home to fight wars all over the world.

At the end of the Cold War, there was a brief reprise when the Right in this country remembered its roots in noninterventionism. But this did not last long. George Bush the First rekindled the militarist spirit with the first war on Iraq, and there has been no fundamental questioning of the American empire ever since. Even today, Republicans elicit their biggest applause by whipping up audiences about foreign threats, while never mentioning that the real threat to American well-being exists in the Beltway.

THE FUTURE

I can think of no greater priority today than a serious and effective antifascist alliance. In many ways, one is already forming. It is not a formal alliance. It is made up of those who protest the Fed, those who refuse to go along with mainstream fascist politics, those who seek decentralization, those who demand lower taxes and free trade, those who seek the right to associate with anyone they want and buy and sell on terms of their own choosing, those who insist they can educate their children on their own, the investors and savers who make economic growth possible, those who do not want to be felt up at airports, and those who have become expatriates.

It is also made of the millions of independent entrepreneurs who are discovering that the number one threat to their ability to serve others through the commercial marketplace is the institution that claims to be our biggest benefactor: the government.

How many people fall into this category? It is more than we know. The movement is intellectual. It is political. It is cultural. It is technological. They come from all classes, races, countries, and professions. This is no longer a national movement. It is truly global.

We can no longer predict whether members consider themselves to be left wing, right wing, independent, libertarian, anarchist, or something else. It includes those as diverse as homeschooling parents in the suburbs as well as parents in urban areas whose children are among the 2.3 million people who languish in jail for no good reason in a country with the largest prison population in the world.

And what does this movement want? Nothing more or less than sweet liberty. It does not ask that the liberty be granted or given. It only asks for the liberty that is promised by life itself and would otherwise exist were it not for the Leviathan state that robs us, badgers us, jails us, kills us.

This movement is not departing. We are daily surrounded by evidence that it is right and true. Every day, it is more and more obvious that the state contributes absolutely nothing to our well-being; it massively subtracts from it.

Back in the 1930s, and even up through the 1980s, the partisans of the state were overflowing with ideas. They had theories and agendas that had many intellectual backers. They were thrilled and excited about the world they would create. They would end business cycles, bring about social advance, build the middle class, cure disease, bring about universal security, and much more. Fascism believed in itself.

This is no longer true. Fascism has no new ideas, no big projects—and not even its partisans really believe it can accomplish what it sets out to do. The world created by the private sector is so much more useful and beautiful than anything the state has done that the fascists have themselves become demoralized and aware that their agenda has no real intellectual foundation.

It is ever more widely known that statism does not and cannot work. Statism is the great lie. Statism gives us the exact opposite of its promise. It promised security, prosperity, and peace; it has given us fear, poverty, war, and death. If we want a future, it is one that we have to build ourselves. The fascist state will not give it to us. On the contrary, it stands in the way.

It also seems to me that the old-time romance of the classical liberals with the idea of the limited state is gone. It is far more likely today that young people embrace an idea that 50 years ago was thought to be unthinkable: the idea that society is best off without any state at all.

I would mark the rise of anarcho-capitalist theory as the most dramatic intellectual shift in my adult lifetime. Gone is that view of the state as the night watchman that would only guard essential rights, adjudicate disputes, and protect liberty.

This view is woefully naive. The night watchman is the guy with the guns, the legal right to use aggression, the guy who controls all comings and goings, the guy who is perched on top and sees all things. Who is watching him? Who is limiting his power? No one, and this is precisely why he is the very source of society's greatest ills. No constitution, no election, no social contract will check his power.

Indeed, the night watchman has acquired total power. It is he who would be the total state, which Flynn describes as a government that "possesses the power to enact any law or take any measure that seems proper to it." So long as a government, he says, "is clothed with the power to do anything without any limitation on its powers, it is totalitarian. It has total power."

It is no longer a point that we can ignore. The night watchman must be removed and his powers distributed within and among the whole population, and they should be governed by the same forces that bring us all the blessings the material world affords us.

In the end, this is the choice we face: the total state or total freedom. Which will we choose? If we choose the state, we will continue to sink further and further and eventually lose all that we treasure as a civilization. If we choose freedom, we can harness that remarkable power of human cooperation that will enable us to continue to make a better world.

In the fight against fascism, there is no reason to be despairing. We must continue to fight with every bit of confidence that the future belongs to us and not them.

Their world is falling apart. Ours is just being built.

Their world is based on bankrupt ideologies. Ours is rooted in the truth about freedom and reality.

Their world can only look back to the glory days. Ours looks forward to the future we are building for ourselves.

Their world is rooted in the corpse of the nation-state. Our world draws on the energies and creativity of all peoples in the world, united in the great and noble project of creating a prospering civilization through peaceful human cooperation.

It's true that they have the biggest guns. But big guns have not assured permanent victory in Iraq or Afghanistan—or any other place on the planet.

We possess the only weapon that is truly immortal: the right idea. It is this that will lead to victory.

As Mises said,

> In the long run even the most despotic governments with all their brutality and cruelty are no match for ideas. Eventually the ideology that has won the support of the majority will prevail and cut the ground from under the tyrant's feet. Then the oppressed many will rise in rebellion and overthrow their masters.

CHAPTER 3

Machiavelli
and State Power*

As libertarianism has acquired a higher profile in American life over the past several years, the attacks on and caricatures of libertarians have grown almost as rapidly. Libertarians, we read, are antisocial, and prefer isolation over interaction with others. They are greedy, and are unmoved if the poor should starve. They are naïve about our dangerous enemies, and refuse their patriotic duty to support the government's wars.

These caricatures and misconceptions can be put to rest by simply defining what libertarianism is. The libertarian idea is based on a fundamental moral principle: nonaggression. No one may initiate physical force against anyone else.

There is nothing antisocial about that. To the contrary, it is the denial of this principle that is antisocial, for it is peaceful interaction that lies at the heart of civilized society.

At first glance, hardly anyone can object to the nonaggression principle. Few people openly support acts of aggression against peaceful parties. But libertarians apply this principle across the board, to all actors, public and private. Our view goes well beyond merely suggesting that the State may not engage in gross violations of the moral law. We contend that the

---

*From a talk delivered on September 15, 2012, at a seminar sponsored by the Columbia University Department of Italian in association with the Mises Institute.

State may not perform any action that would be forbidden to an individual. Moral norms either exist or they do not.

Thus we cannot abide State kidnapping, just because they call it the draft. We cannot abide the incarceration of people who ingest the wrong substances, just because they call it the war on drugs. We cannot abide theft just because they call it taxation. And we cannot abide mass murder just because they call it foreign policy.

Murray Rothbard, who earned his Ph.D. from this very institution (Columbia University) in 1956 and went on to become known as Mr. Libertarian, said that you could discover the libertarian position on any issue by imagining a criminal gang carrying out the action in question.

In other words, libertarianism takes certain moral and political insights shared by a great many people, and simply applies them consistently.

For example, people oppose monopoly because they fear the increase in prices, the decrease in product quality, and the centralization of power that accompany it.

The libertarian applies this concern for monopoly to the State itself. After all, private firms, which we are supposed to fear, can't simply charge whatever they want for their goods or services. Consumers can simply switch from one supplier to another, or from a particular product to a close substitute. Firms cannot engage in quality deterioration without likewise losing customers, who can find competitors offering better products.

But the State may, by definition, charge the public whatever it likes for the so-called services it supplies. Its subjects must accept whatever level of quality the State should deign to provide. And there can never, by definition, be any competitor to the State, since the State is defined as the territorial monopolist of compulsion and coercion.

With its wars, its genocides, and its totalitarian atrocities, the State has proven itself by far the most lethal institution in history. Its lesser crimes include the debt crises it has caused, the self-perpetuating bureaucracies that feed off the productive population, and the squandering of resources—which might otherwise have improved the general standard of living through capital formation—on arbitrary and politically motivated projects.

Yet the State, despite its failures, is consistently given a benefit of the doubt that no one would extend to actors and firms in the private sector. For instance, educational outcomes remain dismal despite vastly increased expenditures and far lower class sizes than in the past. Had the private sector presided over such a disaster, we would never hear the end of all the denunciations of the malefactors of great wealth who are keeping our children ignorant. When the government sector performs so poorly, there is silence. Silence, that is, interrupted by demands that the State be given still more resources.

Years ago, when John Chubb of the Brookings Institution tried to uncover how many bureaucrats were employed in New York City's public school system, it took six telephone calls to reach someone who knew the answer—and that person was not allowed to disclose the information. It took another half dozen calls to find someone who both knew the answer and could reveal it. The answer? Six thousand.

Chubb then called the Archdiocese of New York to find out how many bureaucrats were employed in the administration of the city's Catholic schools, which educated one-sixth as many students. When the first person he called didn't know the answer, he figured he was in for it again. But that person went on to say, "Wait, let me count." It was twenty-six.

Imagine if the situation were reversed, and the top-heavy school system had been the private one. There would be no end to the investigations, the media reports, the public outrage. But when the State is the guilty party, there is no interest in the story at all, and no one even hears about it.

Likewise, when the government courts force innocent parties to endure interminable delays and endless expense, there are no investigations or cries for justice. When the rich and famous are obviously favored by the system, people glumly accept it as a fact of life. Meanwhile, private arbitration companies are flourishing, quietly filling the gap left by the government's awful system—and hardly anyone notices or cares, much less appreciates these improvements in our welfare.

The US government has carried out atrocities of an unspeakable kind, just in the past ten years, and justified them with propaganda claims that nobody around the world, apart from a gullible sector of the American population, took seriously. If K-Mart had somehow managed to do such a thing, everyone involved would have been roundly condemned, and the perpetrators would have been imprisoned, if not executed.

The government, on the other hand, persuades the people that they and the government are the same thing, that the government's wars are their wars, that these conflicts involve us against them. People's moral compasses become blurred as they begin to identify themselves and their own personal goodness, as they see it, with the wars in which "their" government is engaged.

In fact, for the libertarian, the government's wars are not us versus them. The wars are a case of them versus them.

The other side of the Austro-libertarian coin is, of course, the Austrian School of economics.

The Austrian School has enjoyed a renaissance of sorts since the Panic of 2008, since so many economists who belong to this venerable tradition of thought predicted the crisis—in the face of official assurances to the contrary, in the media, among the political class, and from the Federal Reserve itself. Thanks to the Internet, it was impossible for official opinion to black out these dissident voices.

The Austrian School, which was born officially with Carl Menger's 1871 book *Principles of Economics*, is sometimes conflated with other schools of thought loosely associated with the free market. But in its method, its price theory, its monopoly theory, its capital theory, its business-cycle theory, and in so much else, it is distinct from those other schools of thought, and often in direct opposition to them.

It is solidly realistic, and grounded in the individual actor and his decisions and preferences. It seeks to understand real-world prices, not the prices of a long-run equilibrium that can never exist except in the minds of economists.

It was the Austrians who solved problems that had vexed the classical economists, whose price theory could not account for why water, so necessary to life, commanded virtually a zero price on the market, while diamonds, a mere luxury, were so dear.

And it is the Austrians who predicted the Great Depression at a time when fashionable opinion claimed the business cycle had been tamed forever, who predicted the dot-com crash when Fed chairman Alan Greenspan was saying that perhaps booms didn't necessarily have to be followed by busts any longer, and who, as I mentioned, predicted the most recent crisis when the regulators whom we are supposed to trust to keep the economy stable said there was no housing bubble and the fundamentals of that market were sound.

A common caricature holds that supporters of the free market believe the market yields a perfect social outcome, whatever that is supposed to mean. In a world of uncertainty and constant change, no system can yield a perfect result. No system can ensure that the whole structure of production instantaneously adjusts to precisely that allocation of capital goods that will yield the exact array of types and quantities of consumer goods that the public desires, while imposing the least cost in terms of opportunities foregone.

Our point is that no competing system can do a better job than the market. Only actors on the market can allocate resources in a non-arbitrary way, because only on the market can someone evaluate a course of action according to the economizing principle of profit and loss. This is what the Austrians call *economic calculation*.

This was the reason, economist Ludwig von Mises explained in 1920, that socialism could not work. Under socialism as traditionally understood, the State owned the means of production. Now if the State already owns all those things, then no buying and selling of them takes place. Without buying and selling, in turn, there is no process by which prices can arise. And without prices for capital goods, central planners cannot allocate resources rationally. They cannot know whether a particular production process should use ten units of plastic and nine units of lumber, or ten units of lumber and nine units of plastic (if we are indifferent between the two combinations from a technological point of view). Without market prices by which to compare incommensurable goods like lumber and plastic, they cannot know how urgently demanded each input is in alternative lines of production. Multiply this problem by the nearly infinite set of possible combinations of productive factors, and you see the impossible situation the central planning board faces.

Even the non-socialist State has a calculation problem. Since it operates without a profit-and-loss feedback mechanism, it has no way of knowing whether it has allocated resources in accordance with consumer preferences and in a least-cost manner. To the contrary, its decisions regarding what to produce and where, in what quantities and using which methods are completely blind from the point of view of social economizing. (By "social economizing" I mean the process by which we attain higher-valued ends with lower-valued means.)

Hence if we want to ensure that resources are not squandered or spent arbitrarily, we must keep them out of the hands of the State.

Strictly speaking, the Austrian School of economics has nothing to do with libertarianism. Economics, insisted economist Ludwig von Mises, is value-free. It describes rather than prescribes. It does not tell us what we ought to do. It merely explains the various phenomena we observe, from prices to interest rates, and supplies the cause-and-effect analysis that permits us to understand the consequences of coercive interference in the voluntary buying and selling decisions of individuals.

All the same, the knowledge the Austrian School imparts to us strongly implies that certain courses of action are more desirable from the standpoint of human welfare than others. Among other things, we learn from Austrian economics that the State's allocation decisions cannot be socially economizing. We learn that the desires of consumers are best served by the free price system, which directs production decisions up and down the capital structure in accordance with society's demands. And we learn that the State's interference with money, the commodity that forms one-half of every non-barter exchange, gives rise to the devastation of the boom-bust business cycle.

Austro-libertarianism, then, in the spirit of Rothbard, takes the libertarian nonaggression principle and supplements it with the Austrian School's descriptions of the free and unhampered market economy. The result is an elegant and compelling way of understanding the world, which in turn conveys the moral and material urgency of establishing a free society.

Now the seminar today asks us to consider questions of power and the State from an Austro-libertarian perspective, but also in light of Nicolo Machiavelli, the late fifteenth- and early sixteenth-century historian, political theorist, and counselor to princes. Most people know of Machiavelli for the views expressed in his short manual *The Prince*, and not for his longer and perhaps more substantial works, including his *Discourses on Livy* and his history of Florence. I have drawn largely but not exclusively from *The Prince* for my brief remarks today.

The Roman moralists of antiquity, and the Renaissance humanists who followed them, had urged that rulers had to possess a particular set of moral virtues. These were, first, the four cardinal virtues—cardinal from the Latin meaning "hinge"; hence all other virtues hinge on these—of courage, justice, temperance, and wisdom. Now all men were called to cultivate these virtues, but princes in particular were called to still others beyond these, such as princely magnanimity and liberality. These themes are developed in Cicero's *De Officiis*, or *On Duties*, and in Seneca's *On Clemency and On Benefits*.

The humanists anticipated the thesis Machiavelli would one day bring forth, namely that there ought to be a division between morality on the one hand and whatever happens to be expedient for the prince on the other. They answered it by cautioning that even if princely wickedness is not punished in this life, divine retribution in the next life would be fearsome and certain.

What made Machiavelli stand out so starkly was his radical departure from this traditional view of the prince's moral obligations. As the great Machiavelli scholar Quentin Skinner points out, "When we turn to *The Prince* we find this aspect of humanist morality suddenly and violently overturned."

The prince, says Machiavelli, must always "be prepared to act immorally when this becomes necessary." And "in order to maintain his power," he will—not just sometimes but often—be forced "to act treacherously, ruthlessly, and inhumanely."

Most people will never interact with the prince themselves, hence Machiavelli's note to the prince that "everyone can see what you appear to be" but "few have direct experience of what you really are." "A skillful deceiver," he continued, "always finds plenty of people who will let themselves be deceived." We can surmise from this what kind of person the prince would have to be.

It is customary to object at this point that Machiavelli counseled that the prince pursue virtue when possible, and that he should not pursue evil for its own sake. Machiavelli does indeed make such an argument in chapter 15 of *The Prince*. But on the other hand, Machiavelli says that conduct considered virtuous by traditional morality and the general run of mankind merely "seems virtuous," and that apparently wicked behavior that maintains one's power only seems vicious.

Skinner poses, and answers, the historian's natural question when faced with these moral claims:

> But what of the Christian objection that this is a foolish as well as a wicked position to adopt, since it forgets the day of judgment on which all injustices will finally be punished? About this Machiavelli says nothing at all. His silence is eloquent, indeed epoch-making; it echoed around Christian Europe, at first eliciting a stunned silence in return, and then a howl of execration that has never finally died away.

Machiavelli's view has sometimes been summarized as "the ends justify the means." Such a distillation does not capture all aspects of Machiavelli's thought, and no doubt this pithy summary irritates professors of political theory. But if the end in mind is the preservation of the prince's power, then "the ends justify the means" is not an unfair description of Machiavelli's counsel.

This principle, in turn, is what the collectivist State now appeals to in order to justify its own deviations from what people would otherwise consider moral and good. F.A. Hayek wrote, "The principle that the end justifies the means is in individualist ethics regarded as the denial of all morals. In collectivist ethics it becomes necessarily the supreme rule; there is literally nothing which the consistent collectivist must not be prepared to do if it serves 'the good of the whole,' because the 'good of the whole' is to him the only criterion of what ought to be done." Collectivist ethics, he added, "knows no other limit than that set by expediency—the suitability of the particular act for the end in view."

Almost everyone now accepts, at least implicitly, the claim that a different set of moral rules applies to the State, or that to one degree or another the State is above morality as traditionally understood. Even if they would not use some of the verbal formulations of Machiavelli, at some level they believe it is unreasonable to expect the State or its functionaries to behave the way rest of us do. The State may preserve itself by methods that no private business, or household, or organization, or individual would be allowed to employ for their own preservation. We accept this as normal.

This is merely a more general statement of the phenomenon I described earlier, whereby few people even bat an eye when the State engages in behavior that would be considered a moral enormity if carried out by any other person or entity.

Now it will be objected that the coercive apparatus of the State is so important to the right ordering of society that we cannot insist too strongly on libertarian purity when evaluating its behavior. Sometimes the State just has to do what it has to do.

Every so-called service the State provides has in the past been provided non-coercively. We are simply not encouraged to learn this history, and the framework we unknowingly adopt from our earliest days in school makes our imaginations too narrow to conceive of it.

Machiavelli launched one revolution, on behalf of the State. Ours is the revolution against it, and in favor of peace, freedom, and prosperity.

CHAPTER 4

Headed to
National Socialism*

I t was common on the Left to intimate that George W. Bush was like Hitler, a remark that would drive the *National Review* crowd through the
roof but which I didn't find entirely outrageous. Bush's main method of
governance was to stir up fear of foreign enemies and instigate a kind
of nationalist hysteria about the need for waging war and giving up liberty
through security.

Hitler is the most famous parallel here, but he is hardly the only one.
Many statesmen in world history have used the same tactics, dating back
to ancient times. Machiavelli wrote in his *Art of War* advice to the ruler:

> To know how to recognize an opportunity in war, and take it,
> benefits you more than anything else.

But what's the point of studying Hitler's rise to power unless it is to
learn from that history and apply the lessons? One lesson is to beware of
leaders who come to power in troubled times, and then use foreign threats
and economic crises to bolster their own power. Unless we can draw out
lessons for our own times, history becomes nothing but a series of dry data
points with no broader relevance.

Certainly Bush used 9-11 to consolidate his power and the neoconservative intellectuals who surrounded him adopted a deep cynicism concerning

---

*July 10, 2009

the manipulation of public opinion. Their governing style concerned the utility of public myth, which they found essential to wise rule. The main myth they promoted was that Bush was the Christian philosopher-king heading a new crusade against Islamic extremism. The very stupid among us believed it, and this served as a kind of ideological infrastructure of his tenure as president.

Then it collapsed when the economy went south and he was unable to sustain the absurd idea that he was protecting us from anyone. The result was disgrace, and the empowering of the political left and its socialistic ethos.

The talk of Hitler in the White House ended forthwith, as if the analogy extended only when nationalist ideology is ruling the day. What people don't remember is that Hitlerism was about more than just militarism, nationalism, and consolidation of identity politics. It also involved a substantial shift in German domestic politics away from free enterprise, or what remained of it under Weimar, toward collectivist economic planning.

Nazism was not only nationalism run amok. It was also socialism of a particular variety.

Let's turn to *The Vampire Economy* by Guenter Reimann (1939). He begins the story with the 1933 decree that all property must be subject to the collective will. It began with random audits and massive new bookkeeping regulations:

> Manufacturers in Germany were panic-stricken when they heard of the experiences of some industrialists who were more or less expropriated by the State. These industrialists were visited by State auditors who had strict orders to "examine" the balance sheets and all bookkeeping entries of the company (or individual businessman) for the preceding two, three, or more years until some error or false entry was found. The slightest formal mistake was punished with tremendous penalties. A fine of millions of marks was imposed for a single bookkeeping error. Obviously, the examination of the books was simply a pretext for partial expropriation of the private capitalist with a view to complete expropriation and seizure of the desired property later. The owner of the property was helpless, since under fascism there is no longer an independent judiciary that protects the property rights of private citizens against the State. The authoritarian State has made it a principle that private property is no longer sacred.

WHAT A GERMAN AUTO MANUFACTURER HAS TO DO TO GET 5,000 TIRES FOR HIS CARS

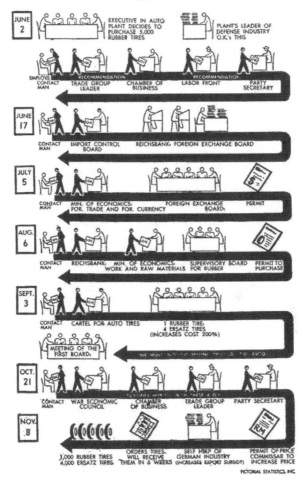

The rules begin to change slowly so that enterprise could no longer make decisions in the interest of profitability. The banks were nationalized. The heads of major companies were changed. Hiring and firing became heavily politicized. The courts ruled not on justice but on political priorities. It was no longer enough merely to obey the laws. The national will must trump economic concerns:

> The capitalist under fascism has to be not merely a law-abiding citizen, he must be servile to the representatives of the State. He

must not insist on "rights" and must not behave as if his private property rights were still sacred. He should be grateful to the Fuehrer that he still has private property. This state of affairs must lead to the final collapse of business morale, and sound the death knell of the self-respect and self-reliance which marked the independent businessman under liberal capitalism.

Price controls were next, enforced intermittently and with them grew up a large gray economy, with businesspeople spending more time getting around the rules than producing wealth.

To increase his prices a dealer must have a special permit from the Price Commissar. A request for a price increase must first be certified to by the group leader; it must be accompanied by a detailed statement of necessity and other pertinent data, such as production and distribution costs.

State production mandates were next. Goods were to be produced according to political goals.

Backed by the General Staff of the army, Nazi bureaucrats have been able to embark upon schemes which compel the most powerful leaders of business and finance to undertake projects which they consider both risky and unprofitable.

Bankers were required to act as state actors.

Under fascism, big bankers, formerly independent—except, of course, "non-Aryans"—have become State officials in everything but name. They are often in high and influential positions, but they are all members of the compact, centralized State machine. Their independence, their individual initiative, their free competitive position, all the principles for which they once fought fervently, are gone.

If you think that the parallels stopped after Bush left power, consider this passage from Reimann:

The totalitarian State reverses the former relationship between the State and the banks. Previously, their political influence increased when the State needed financial help. Now the opposite holds true. The more urgent the financial demands of the State become, the stricter measures are taken by the State in order to compel these institutions to invest their funds as the State may wish.

Once the banks were forced wholly under the control of the government, they became the means by which all property became subject to the state:

> The totalitarian State will not have an empty treasury so long as private companies or individuals still have ample cash or liquid assets. For the State has the power to solve its financial difficulties at their expense. The private banks themselves, the financial institutions which previously dictated the terms on which they were willing to lend money, have built up the system of siphoning off liquid funds. This financial system is now utilized by the totalitarian State for its own purposes.

So it was for the stock market, which was regarded as a national asset. Speculation was forbidden. Public companies were entirely subject to bureaucratic rule. Order replaced the old spontaneity, while speculation of the old sort became an entirely underground activity. The largest companies didn't entirely mind the course of events.

> The disappearance of small corporations gives rise to a tendency among small investors not to risk their capital in new competitive enterprises. The larger the big corporations grow and the closer they become connected with the State bureaucracy, the fewer chances there are for the rise of new competitors.

So too for insurance companies, which were compelled to buy government paper.

The tendency toward ever more economic regulation resulted not in socialism as such but fascist planning.

> The fascist State does not merely grant the private entrepreneur the right to produce for the market, but insists on production as a duty which must be fulfilled even though there be no profit. The businessman cannot close down his factory or shop because he finds it unprofitable. To do this requires a special permit issued by the authorities.

The national demand for "stimulus" replaced private decision making entirely, as businessmen were required to produce and avoid any economic downturns that might embarrass the state.

> The Nazi government has expressly threatened the private entrepreneur with increased State coercion and reduction of personal rights and liberties unless he fulfills adequately the "duty to produce" according to the State's demands.

But stimulus could not and would not work, no matter how hard the party officials tried, because the very institutions of private property and competition and all market forces had been overwritten.

> The totalitarian regime has annihilated the most important conservative force of capitalism, the belief that private property ought to be a sacred right of every citizen and that the private property of every citizen ought to be protected. Respect for private property has penetrated the spirit of the people in all capitalist countries. It is the strongest bulwark of capitalism. Fascism has succeeded in destroying this conservative force. . . . People still have to work for money and have to live on money incomes. Possession of capital still provides income. But this income is largely at the mercy of State bureaucrats and Party officials.

Reimann sums up:

> In Nazi Germany there is no field of business activity in which the State does not interfere. In more or less detailed form it prescribes how the businessman may use capital which is still presumably his private property. And because of this, the German businessman has become a fatalist; he does not believe that the new rules will work out well, yet he knows that he cannot alter the course of events. He has been made the tool of a gigantic machine which he cannot direct.

The regime also dramatically increased social and medical legislation, providing lifetime pensions to friends and conscripting doctors in the service of its dietary and medical goals.

Now, if any of this sounds familiar, it is because the principles of intervention are universal.

The Nazi regime represented not a unique evil in history but rather a now-conventional combination of two dangerous ideological trends: nationalism and socialism.

We know both all too well.

CHAPTER 5

The Dawn of Late Fascism*

The downgrading of US debt this summer didn't have huge economic consequences, but the psychological ones were truly devastating for the national elites who have run this country for nearly a century. For a State that regards itself as infallible, it was a huge blow that market forces delivered against the government, and it is only one of thousands that have cut against the power elite in recent years.

Another recent example was the vanishing of the much-vaunted Obama jobs bill. He pushed hard for this scheme for a month. He made an FDR-like national speech that attempted to whip up a public frenzy. He promised that if the legislature passed his law, supply and demand for workers would magically come together. We only need to agree to spend a few hundred billion more!

Well, the bully pulpit has become the bull-something pulpit. It seems that hardly anyone even took the speech seriously as a political point. It was reviewed and treated as the theater that it was, but the universal reaction to the specifics was a thumbs down, even from his own party.

No, Obama is not FDR. This is not the New Deal. The public will not be browbeaten as it once was. The polls show a vast lack of even a modicum of confidence in political leadership, the failures of which are all around us.

---

*October 15, 2011

41

The longer the depression persists, the more the rebellious spirit grows, and it is not limited to the Wall Street protests. Poverty is growing, incomes are falling, business is being squeezed at every turn, and unemployment is stuck at intolerably high levels. People are angry as never before, and neither political party comes close to offering answers.

The State as we've known it—and that includes its political parties and its redistributionary, military, regulatory, and money-creating bureaucracies—just can't get it together. It's as true now as it has been for some twenty years: the Nation State is in precipitous decline. Once imbued with grandeur and majesty, personified by its Superman powers to accomplish amazing global feats, it is now a wreck and out of ideas.

It doesn't seem that way because the State is more in-your-face than it has been in all of American history. We see the State at the airport with the incompetent bullying ways of the TSA. We see it in the ridiculous dinosaur of the post office, forever begging for more money so it can continue to do things the way it did them in 1950. We see it in the federalized cops in our towns, once seen as public servants but now revealed as what they have always been: armed tax collectors, censors, spies, thugs.

These are themselves marks of decline. The mask of the State is off. And it has been off for such a long time that we can hardly remember what it looked like when it was on.

So let's take a quick tour. If you live in a big metropolitan city, drive to the downtown post office (if it is still standing). There you will find a remarkable piece of architecture, tall and majestic and filled with grandeur. There is a liberal use of Roman-style columns. The ceilings indoors are extremely high and thrilling. It might even be the biggest and most impressive building around.

This is a building of an institution that believed in itself. After all, this was the institution that carried the mail, which was the only way that people had to communicate with each other when most of these places were first erected. The state took great pride in offering this service, which it held up as being superior to anything the market could ever provide (even if market provisions like the Pony Express had to be outlawed). Postmen were legendary (or so we were told) for their willingness to brave the elements to bring us the essential thing we needed in life apart from food, clothing, and shelter.

And today? Look at the thing that we call the post office. It is a complete wreck, a national joke, a hanger-on from a day long gone. They deliver physical spam to our mail boxes, and a few worthwhile things every once in a while, but the only time they are in the news is when we hear another report of their bankruptcy and need for a bailout.

It's the same with all the grand monuments of yesteryear's statism. Think of the Hoover Dam, Mount Rushmore, the endless infrastructure projects of the New Deal, the Eisenhower interstate highway system, the moon shot, the sprawling monuments to itself that the State has erected from sea to shining sea. As I've explained elsewhere, these all came about in an age when the only real alternative to socialism was considered to be fascism. This was an age when freedom—as in the old-fashioned sense—was just out of the question.

The State in all times and all places operates by force—and force alone. But the style of rule changes. The fascist style emphasized inspiration, magnificence, industrial progress, grandeur, all headed by a valiant leader making smart decisions about all things. This style of American rule lasted from the New Deal through the end of the Cold War.

But this whole system of inspiration has nearly died out. In the communist tradition of naming the stages of history, we can call this late fascism. The fascist system in the end cannot work because, despite the claims, the State does not have the means to achieve what it promises. It does not possess the capability to outrun private markets in technology, of serving the population in the way markets can, of making things more plentiful or cheaper, or even of providing basic services in a manner that is economically efficient.

Fascism, like socialism, cannot achieve its aims. So there is a way in which it makes sense to speak of a stage of history: We are in the stage of late fascism. The grandeur is gone, and all we are left with is a gun pointed at our heads. The system was created to be great, but it is reduced in our time to being crude. Valor is now violence. Majesty is now malice.

Consider whether there is any national political leader in power today the death of whom would call forth anywhere near the same level of mourning as the death of Steve Jobs. People know in their hearts who serves them, and it is not the guy with jackboots, tasers on his belt, and a federal badge. The time when we looked to this man as a public servant is long gone. And this reality only speeds the inevitable death of the State as the 20th century re-invented it.

CHAPTER 6

The US Corporate State*

I t didn't take long for opponents of the market to pounce after the events of 2008. The crash was said to prove how destructive "unregulated capitalism" could be and how dangerous its supporters were—after all, free-marketeers opposed the bailouts, which had allegedly saved Americans from another Great Depression.

In *The Great Deformation*, David Stockman—former US congressman and budget director under Ronald Reagan—tells the story of the recent crisis, and takes direct aim at the conventional wisdom that credits government policy and Ben Bernanke with rescuing Americans from another Great Depression. In this he has made a seminal contribution. But he does much more than this. He offers a sweeping, revisionist account of US economic history from the New Deal to the present. He refutes widely held myths about the Reagan years and the demise of the Soviet Union. He covers the growth and expansion of the warfare state. He shows precisely how the Fed enriches the powerful and shelters them from free markets. He demonstrates the flimsiness of the present so-called recovery. Above all, he shows that attempts to blame our economic problems on "capitalism" are preposterous, and reveal a complete lack of understanding of how the economy has been deformed over the past several decades.

---

*March 2, 2013

45

The Great Deformation takes on the stock arguments in favor of the bailouts that we heard in 2008 and which constitute the conventional wisdom even today. A "contagion effect" would spread the financial crisis throughout the economy, well beyond the confines of a few Wall Street firms, we were told. Without bailouts, payroll would not be met. ATMs would go dark. Wise policy decisions by the Treasury and the Fed prevented these and other nightmare scenarios, and staved off a second Great Depression.

The bailout of AIG, for example, was carried out against a backdrop of utter hysteria. AIG was bailed out in order to protect Main Street, the public was told, but virtually none of AIG's busted CDS insurance was held by Main Street banks. Even on Wall Street the effects were confined to about a dozen firms, every one of which had ample cushion for absorbing the losses. Thanks to the bailout, they did not take one dollar in such losses. "The bailout," says Stockman, "was all about protecting short-term earnings and current-year executive and trader bonuses."

Ten years earlier, the Fed had sent a clear enough signal of its future policy when it arranged for a bailout of a hedge fund called Long Term Capital Management (LTCM). If *this* firm was to be bailed out, Wall Street concluded, then there was no limit to the madness the Fed would backstop with easy money.

LTCM, says Stockman, was

> an egregious financial train wreck that had amassed leverage ratios of 100 to 1 in order to fund giant speculative bets in currency, equity, bond, and derivatives markets around the globe. The sheer recklessness and scale of LTCM's speculations had no parallel in American financial history. . . . LTCM stunk to high heaven, and had absolutely no claim on public authority, resources, or even sympathy.

When the S&P 500 soared by 50 percent over the next fifteen months, this was not a sign that American companies were seeing their profit outlooks increase by half. It instead indicated a confidence on Wall Street that the Fed would prevent investment errors from receiving the usual free-market punishment. Under this "ersatz capitalism," stock market averages reflected "expected monetary juice from the central bank, not anticipated growth of profits from free-market enterprises."

It wasn't just specific firms that would enjoy Fed largesse under chairmen Alan Greenspan and Ben Bernanke; it was the stock market itself. According to Stockman, Fed policy came to focus on the "wealth effect": if the

Fed pushed stock prices higher, Americans would feel wealthier and would be likely to spend and borrow more, thereby stimulating economic activity.

This policy approach, in turn, practically compelled the bailouts that were one day to come. Anything that might send stock prices lower would frustrate the wealth effect. So the system had to be propped up by whatever means necessary.

What does this policy have to show for itself? Stockman gives the answer:

> If the monetary central planners have been trying to create jobs through the roundabout method of "wealth effects," they ought to be profoundly embarrassed by their incompetence. The only thing that has happened on the job-creation front over the last decade is a massive expansion of the bedpan and diploma mill brigade; that is, employment in nursing homes, hospitals, home health agencies, and for-profit colleges. Indeed, the HES complex accounts for the totality of American job creation since the late 1990s.

Meanwhile, the number of breadwinner jobs did not increase at all between January 2000 and January 2007, remaining at 71.8 million. The booms in housing, the stock market, and household consumption had only this grim statistic to show for themselves. When we consider the entire twelve-year period beginning in the year 2000, there has been a net gain of 18,000 jobs per month—one-eighth of the growth rate in the labor force.

In the wake of the crash, the Fed has continued to gin up the stock market. By September 2012 the S&P had increased by 115 percent over its lows during the bust. Of the 5.6 million breadwinner jobs lost during the correction, only 200,000 had been restored by then. And during the vaunted recovery, American households spent $30 billion less on food and groceries in the fall of 2012 than they did during the same period in 2007.

The sudden emergence of enormous budget deficits in recent years, Stockman explains, simply made manifest what the bubble conditions of the Bush years had concealed. The phony wealth of the housing and consumption booms temporarily lowered the amount of money spent on safety-net programs, and temporarily increased the amount of tax revenue received by the government. With this false prosperity abating, the true deficit, which had simply been suppressed by these temporary factors, began to appear.

All along, the Fed had assured us that the United States was experiencing genuine prosperity. "Flooding Wall Street with easy money," Stockman writes, the Fed

> saw the stock averages soar and pronounced itself pleased with the resulting "wealth effects." Turning the nation's homes into debt-dispensing ATMs, it witnessed a household consumption spree and marveled that the "incoming" macroeconomic data was better than expected. That these deformations were mistaken for prosperity and sustainable economic growth gives witness to the everlasting folly of the monetary doctrines now in vogue in the Eccles Building.

Stockman also discusses the fiscal condition of the U.S. government. Part of that history takes him through the Reagan military buildup. Stockman's isn't the story you heard at the Republican conventions of the 1980s. The real story is as you suspected: a feeding frenzy of arbitrary and irrelevant programs which, once begun, could be stopped only with great difficulty if at all, given the jobs that depended on them.

But at least this buildup brought about the collapse of the Soviet Union, right? Stockman doesn't buy it. "The $3.5 trillion (2005) spent on defense during the Gipper's term did not cause the Kremlin to raise the white flag of surrender. Virtually none of it was spent on programs which threatened Soviet security or undermined its strategic nuclear deterrent."

> At the heart of the Reagan defense buildup . . . was a great double shuffle. The war drums were sounding a strategic nuclear threat that virtually imperiled American civilization. Yet the money was actually being allocated to tanks, amphibious landing craft, close air support helicopters, and a vast conventional armada of ships and planes.
>
> These weapons were of little use in the existing nuclear standoff, but were well suited to imperialistic missions of invasion and occupation. Ironically, therefore, the Reagan defense buildup was justified by an Evil Empire that was rapidly fading but was eventually used to launch elective wars against an Axis of Evil which didn't even exist.

What would actually bring the Soviet Union down was its command economy itself—a point, Stockman notes, that libertarian economists had been making for some time. Neoconservatives, on the other hand, advanced ludicrous claims about Soviet capabilities and the Soviet economy at a time when its decrepitude should have been obvious to everyone.

These inflated claims about the regime's enemies continued to be standard practice for the neocons long after the Reagan years were over.

To do it justice, *The Great Deformation* really requires two or three reviews. One could be devoted just to Stockman's striking analysis of the New Deal. Stockman advances and then defends these and other arguments: the banking system had stabilized well before FDR's ill-advised "bank holiday"; the economy had already turned the corner before FDR's accession and worsened again as a result of FDR's conduct during the interregnum; the New Deal was not a coherent program of Keynesian demand stimulus, so it makes no sense for Keynesians to draw lessons from it; the 1937 "depression within the Depression" was not caused by fiscal retrenchment; and FDR's primary legacy is not the economic recovery, which would have occurred faster without him, but rather the impetus he gave to crony capitalism in one sector of the economy after another.

You may have gathered that *The Great Deformation* must be a long book. It is. But its subject matter is so interesting, and its prose style so lively and engaging, that you will hardly notice the pages going by.

The target of Stockman's book is just about everyone in the political and media establishments. Left-liberal opinion molders—defenders of the common man, they would have us believe—supported the bailouts in overwhelming numbers. Herman Cain, meanwhile, lectured "free-market purists" for opposing TARP, and virtually the entire slate of GOP candidates in 2012 had supported it. Both sides, in tandem with the official media, repeated the regime's scare stories without cavil. And both sides could think of nothing but good things to say about how the Fed had managed the economy for the past quarter century.

The free market stands exonerated of the charges hurled by the state and its allies.

Thanks to *The Great Deformation*, not a shred of the regime's propaganda is left standing. This is truly the book we have been waiting for, and we owe David Stockman a great debt.

Capitalism and Its Heroes

CHAPTER 7

The World of Salamanca*

The subject of the medieval period highlights the vast gulf that separates scholarly opinion from popular opinion. This is a grave frustration for scholars who have been working to change popular opinion for a hundred years. For most people, the medieval period brings to mind populations living by myths and crazy superstitions such as we might see in a Monty Python skit. Scholarly opinion, however, knows otherwise. The age between the 8th and 16th centuries was a time of amazing advance in every area of knowledge, such as architecture, music, biology, mathematics, astronomy, industry, and—yes—economics.

One might think it would be enough to look at the Burgos Cathedral of St. Mary, begun in 1221 and completed nine years later, to know there is something gravely wrong with the popular wisdom.

The popular wisdom comes through in the convention among non-specialists to trace the origins of promarket thinking to Adam Smith (1723–1790). The tendency to see Smith as the fountainhead of economics is reinforced among Americans, because his famed book *An Inquiry into the Nature and Causes of the Wealth of Nations* was published in the year America seceded from Britain.

There is much this view of intellectual history overlooks. The real founders of economic science actually wrote hundreds of years before

---

*October 27, 2009

Smith. They were not economists as such, but moral theologians, trained in the tradition of St. Thomas Aquinas, and they came to be known as the Late Scholastics. These men, most of whom taught in Spain, were at least as pro–free market as the much-later Scottish tradition. Plus, their theoretical foundation was even more solid: they anticipated the theories of value and price of the "marginalists" of late 19th-century Austria.

The scholar who rediscovered the Late Scholastics for the English-speaking world was Raymond de Roover (1904–1972). For years, they had been ridiculed and sloughed off, and even called presocialists in their thought. Karl Marx was the "last of the Schoolmen," wrote R. H. Tawney. But de Roover demonstrated that nearly all the conventional wisdom was wrong (Julius Kirchner ed., *Business, Banking, and Economic Thought* [Chicago: University of Chicago Press, 1974]).

Joseph Schumpeter gave the Late Scholastics a huge boost with his posthumously published 1954 book, *History of Economic Analysis* (New York: Oxford University Press). "It is they," he wrote, "who come nearer than does any other group to having been the 'founders' of scientific economics."

About the same time, there appeared a book of readings put together by Marjorie Grice-Hutchinson (*The School of Salamanca* [Oxford: Clarendon Press, 1952]), recently republished by the Mises Institute. A full-scale interpretive work appeared later (*Early Economic Thought in Spain, 1177–1740* [London: Allen & Unwin, 1975]).

In our own time, Alejandro Chafuen (*Christians for Freedom* [San Francisco: Ignatius Press, 1986]) linked the Late Scholastics closely with the Austrian School. In the fullest and most important treatment to date, Murray N. Rothbard's *An Austrian Perspective on the History of Economic Thought* (London: Edward Elgar, 1995) presents the extraordinarily wide range of Late Scholastic thought. Rothbard offers an explanation for the widespread misinterpretation of the School of Salamanca, along with an overarching framework of the intersection between economics and religion from St. Thomas through to the mid-19th century.

What emerges from this growing literature is an awareness that the medieval period was the founding period of economics.

One must recall the opening words of Mises's own *Human Action* here. "Economics is the youngest of all sciences," he announces. "Economics opened to human science a domain previously inaccessible and never thought of."

And what did economics contribute? Mises explains that economics discovered "a regularity in the sequence and interdependence of market phenomena." In so doing, "it conveyed knowledge which could be regarded neither as logic, mathematics, psychology, physics, nor biology."

Let me pause here with some comments on those who reject outright economics as a science. This tendency is not limited to the Left who embrace the fantasy called socialism, nor the environmentalists who think that society should revert to the status of a hunting and gathering tribe. I'm thinking in particular of a group that we might call conservatives. People who believe that all they need to know about reality and truth is contained in the writings of the ancient philosophers, the Church fathers, or some other time-tested source, whereas anything modern—defined as anything written in the latter half of the 2nd millennium of Christianity—is generally seen as suspect.

This tendency is widespread on the American Right, and extends to the Straussians, the communitarians, the paleoconservatives, and the religious conservatives. There are examples among them all. To seek economic wisdom, they brush aside everything of the last 500 years, and return again and again to the writings of early saints, of Plato and Aristotle, and to words of wisdom from many other revered nonmoderns.

Now, in these writings one can discover great truths. However, it is simply not the case that one can find rigorous economic logic. The writings of this period tend to be imbued with a bias against the merchant, a fallacy about the equality of value in exchange, and a general lack of conviction that there exists a persistent logic for understanding the development of the market.

Mises was right: the development of economics began much later, and the reason for this is rather straightforward. The appearance of widespread economic opportunity, social mobility driven by material status, the dramatic expansion of the division of labor across many borders, and the building of complex capital structures only began to be observed in the late Middle Ages. It was the appearance of the rudimentary structures of modern capitalism that gave rise to the curiosity about economic science. To put it quite simply, it was in the late Middle Ages that there appeared to be something to study at all.

It was in this period on the Continent that we began to see what was previously unheard of: large swaths of the population began to grow rich. Wealth was no longer limited to kings and princes. It was not available only to merchants and bankers. Workers and peasants too could increase their standard of living, make choices about where to live, and acquire clothing and food once reserved for the nobility. In addition, monetary institutions were increasingly complex, with a variety of exchange rates, pressures to permit the paying and charging of interest, and complex investment transactions making their way into daily life.

It was particularly interesting to see wealth being generated in financial services. People who were doing nothing other than arbitraging exchange rates were growing enormously rich and influential. These were people who, in the words of Saravia de la Calle, were "traveling from fair to fair and from place to place with [their] table and boxes and books." And yet their wealth grew and grew. This gave rise to the scientific question of how this was happening. And it also gave rise to the broadest forms of moral questions.

What exactly is the status of the merchant in moral theology? How should this form of moneymaking be regarded by society and the Church? These sorts of questions cried out for answers.

Now let us understand a bit more about the Scholastic mind as shaped in the tradition of St. Thomas. At the root of the Thomist worldview was a conviction that all truth was unified into a single body of thought, and that this truth ultimately pointed to the Author of all truth. Insofar as science was seeking truth, the truth that they found was necessarily reconcilable with other existing truth.

In this way, they saw the idea of truth as operating very much like mathematics. It was integrated from the lowest and most fundamental form to the highest and more elaborate form. If there was a contradiction or a failure to link a higher truth to a lower truth, one could know with certainty that there was something going wrong.

So knowledge was not parceled out and segmented the way it is today. Today, students go to classes on math, literature, economics, and building design, and don't expect to find any links among the disciplines. I'm quite certain that it would never occur to them to try. It is just an accepted aspect of the positivist program that knowledge need not be integrated.

We must all exist in a state of suspended skepticism about everything, and be buffeted about randomly by the latest ideological fad that seems to have some scientific support. The conviction that small truth is related to large truth has been eviscerated.

It is sometimes said that the Scholastics' attitude toward truth made them skeptical toward scientific inquiry. Indeed, the very opposite is true. Their convictions concerning integral truth made them utterly fearless. There was no aspect of life that should escape serious scholarship investigation and exploration.

No matter the findings, if they were true, the investigation could be seen as part of the larger mission of discovering more about God's own creation. There could be no such thing as a dichotomy between science and religion, so one need not hesitate to discover more about either or both.

It is not precisely correct to say that the Late Scholastic thinkers who discovered economics were exploring theological territory and stumbled inadvertently upon economics. They were in fact intensely curious about the logic that governs relations among choices and people in the marketplace, and they looked at this subject without feeling the need to point constantly to theological truth. The relationship between economics and theology was assumed to be a part of the scholarly enterprise itself, and this is why the Late Scholastics could write with such precision on economic subjects.

As Spain, Portugal, and Italy emerged as centers of commerce and enterprise in the 15th and 16th centuries, the universities under the control of the late Thomists spawned a great project of investigating the regular patterns that governed economic life. I would like to present some of these thinkers and their work.

FRANCISCO DE VITORIA

The first of the moral theologians to research, write, and teach at the University of Salamanca was Francisco de Vitoria (1485–1546). Under his guidance, the university offered an extraordinary 70 professorial chairs. As with other great mentors in history, most of Vitoria's published work comes to us in the form of notes taken by his students.

In Vitoria's work on economics, he argued that the just price is the price that has been arrived at by common agreement among producers and consumers. That is, when a price is set by the interplay of supply and demand, it is a just price.

So it is with international trade. Governments should not interfere with the prices and relations established between traders across borders. Vitoria's lectures on Spanish-Indian trade—originally published in 1542 and again in 1917 by the Carnegie Endowment—argued that government intervention with trade violates the Golden Rule.

He also contributed to liberalizing the rule against charging and paying interest. This discussion helped sow a great deal of confusion among theologians of precisely what constituted usury, and this confusion was highly welcome to entrepreneurs. Vitoria was also very careful to take supply and demand into account when analyzing currency exchange.

Yet Vitoria's greatest contribution was producing gifted and prolific students. They went on to explore almost all aspects, moral and theoretical, of economic science. For a century, these thinkers formed a mighty force for free enterprise and economic logic.

They regarded the price of goods and services as an outcome of the actions of traders. Prices vary depending on the circumstance, and depending on the value that individuals place on goods. That value in turn depends on two factors: the goods' availability and their use. The price of goods and services are a result of the operation of these forces. Prices are not fixed by nature, or determined by the costs of production; prices are a result of the common estimation of men.

DOMINGO DE SOTO

Domingo de Soto (1494–1560) was a Dominican priest who became a professor of philosophy at Salamanca. He held powerful positions with the emperor, but chose the academic life. He made important advances in the theory of interest, arguing for a general liberalization.

He was also the architect of the purchasing-parity theory of exchange. He wrote as follows:

> The more plentiful money is in Medina the more unfavorable are the terms of exchange, and the higher the price that must be paid by whoever wishes to send money from Spain to Flanders, since the demand for money is smaller in Spain than in Flanders. And the scarcer money is in Medina the less he need pay there, because more people want money in Medina than are sending it to Flanders.

With these words, he had taken large steps toward justifying the profit that comes from currency arbitrage. It was not by chance that currency valuations come to be; they reflect certain facts on the ground, and the choices of people in light of real scarcities.

He continues:

> It is lawful to exchange money in one place for money in another having regard to its scarcity in the one and abundance in the other, and to receive a smaller sum in a place where money is scarce in exchange for a larger where it is abundant.

Martin de Azpilcueta Navarrus

Another student was Martin de Azpilcueta Navarrus (1493–1586), a Dominican friar, the most prominent canon lawyer of his day, and eventually the adviser to three successive popes. Using reasoning, Navarrus was the first economic thinker to state clearly and unequivocally that government price-fixing is a mistake. When goods are plentiful, there is no need for a set maximum price; when they are not, price control does more harm than good.

In a 1556 manual on moral theology, Navarrus pointed out that it is not a sin to sell goods at higher than the official price when it is agreed to among all parties. Navarrus was also the first to fully state that the quantity of money is a main influence in determining its purchasing power.

"Other things being equal," he wrote in his *Commentary on Usury*, "in countries where there is a great scarcity of money, all other saleable goods, and even the hands and labor of men, are given for less money than where it is abundant." He is generally regarded as the first thinker to observe that the high cost of living is related to the quantity of money.

For a currency to settle at its correct price in terms of other currencies, it is traded at a profit—an activity which was controversial among some theorists on moral grounds. But Navarrus argued that it was not against natural law to trade currencies. This was not the primary purpose of money, but "it is nonetheless an important secondary use."

He used another market good for an analogy. The purpose of shoes, he said, is to protect our feet, but that doesn't mean they shouldn't be traded at a profit. In his view, it would be a terrible mistake to shut down foreign exchange markets, as some people were urging. The result "would be to plunge the realm into poverty."

Diego de Covarrubias y Leiva

The greatest student of Navarrus was Diego de Covarrubias y Leiva (1512–1577), considered the best jurist in Spain since Vitoria. The emperor made him chancellor of Castile, and he eventually became the bishop of Segovia. His book *Variarum* (1554) was then the clearest explanation on the source of economic value. "The value of an article," he said, "does not depend on its essential nature but on the estimation of men, even if that estimation is foolish."

For this reason, the justness of a price is not dictated by how much the item costs or how much labor went into acquiring it. All that matters is what the common market value is in the place and at the time it is sold.

Prices fall when buyers are few and rise when buyers are many. It seems like such a simple point, but it was missed by economists for centuries until the Austrian School rediscovered this "subjective theory of value" and incorporated it into microeconomics.

Like all of these Spanish theorists, Covarrubias believed that individual owners of property had inviolable rights to that property. One of many controversies of the time was whether plants that produce medicines ought to belong to the community. Those who said they should pointed out that the medicine is not a result of any human labor or skill. But Covarrubias said everything that grows on a plot of land should belong to the owner of the land. That owner is even entitled to withhold valuable medicines from the market, and it is a violation of the natural law to force him to sell.

Luis de Molina

Another great economist in the Vitoria line of thinkers was Luis de Molina (1535–1601), who was among the first of the Jesuits to think about theoretical economic topics. Though devoted to the Salamancan School and its achievement, Molina taught in Portugal at the University of Coimbra. He was the author of a five-volume treatise *De Justitia et Jure* (1593 and following). His contributions to law, economics, and sociology were enormous, and his treatise went through several editions.

Among all the pro–free market thinkers of his generation, Molina was most consistent in his view of economic value. Like the other Late Scholastics, he agreed that goods are valued not "according to their nobility or perfection" but according "to their ability to serve human utility." But he provided this compelling example: Rats, according to their nature, are more "noble" (higher up the hierarchy of Creation) than wheat. But rats "are not esteemed or appreciated by men" because "they are of no utility whatsoever."

The use value of a particular good is not fixed between people or over the passage of time. It changes according to individual valuations and availability.

This theory also explains peculiar aspects of luxury goods. For example, why would a pearl, "which can only be used to decorate," be more expensive than grain, wine, meat, or horses? It appears that all these things are more useful than a pearl, and they are certainly more "noble." As Molina explained, valuation is done by individuals, and "we can conclude that the just price for a pearl depends on the fact that some men wanted to grant it value as an object of decoration."

A similar paradox that befuddled the classical economists was the diamond-water paradox. Why should water, which is more useful, be lower in price than diamonds? Following Scholastic logic, it is due to individual valuations and their interplay with scarcity. The failure to understand this point led Adam Smith, among others, off in the wrong direction.

But Molina understood the crucial importance of free-floating prices and their relationship to enterprise. Partly, this was due to Molina's extensive travels and interviews with merchants of all sorts.

"When a good is sold in a certain region or place at a certain price," he observed, so long as it is "without fraud or monopoly or any foul play," then "that price should be held as a rule and measure to judge the just price of said good in that region or place." If the government tries to set a price that is higher or lower, then it would be unjust. Molina was also the first to show why it is that retail prices are higher than wholesale prices: consumers buy in smaller quantities and are willing to pay more for incremental units.

The most sophisticated writings of Molina concerned money and credit. Like Navarrus before him, he understood the relationship of money to prices, and knew that inflation resulted from a higher money supply.

"Just as the abundance of goods causes prices to fall," he wrote (specifying that this assumes the quantity of money and number of merchants remain the same), so too does an "abundance of money" cause prices to rise (again, ceteris paribus). He even went further to point out how wages, income, and even dowries eventually rise in the same proportion to which the money supply increases.

He used this framework to push out the accepted bounds of charging interest, or "usury," a major sticking point for most economists of this period. He argued that it should be permissible to charge interest on any loan involving an investment of capital, even when the return doesn't materialize.

Molina's defense of private property rested on the belief that property is secured in the commandment, "thou shalt not steal." But he went beyond his contemporaries by making strong practical arguments as well. When property is held in common, he said, it won't be taken care of and people will fight to consume it. Far from promoting the public good, when property is not divided, the strong people in the group will take advantage of the weak by monopolizing and consuming the most resources.

Like Aristotle, Molina also thought that common ownership of property would guarantee the end of liberality and charity. But he went further to argue that "alms should be given from private goods and not from the common ones."

In most writings on ethics and sin today, different standards apply to government than to individuals. But not in the writings of Molina. He argued that the king can, as king, commit a variety of mortal sins. For example, if the king grants a monopoly privilege to some, he violates the consumers' right to buy from the cheapest seller. Molina concluded that those who benefit are required by moral law to offset the damages they cause.

Vitoria, Navarrus, Covarrubias, de Soto, and Molina were five of the most important among more than a dozen extraordinary thinkers who had solved difficult economic problems long before the classical period of economics.

Trained in the Thomist tradition, they used logic to understand the world around them, and looked for institutions that would promote prosperity and the common good. It is hardly surprising, then, that many of the Late Scholastics were passionate defenders of the free market and liberty.

THE AUSTRIAN TRADITION

Ideas are like capital in the following sense: we take them for granted, but in fact they are the work of many generations. In the case of economic logic, it was the work of hundreds of years. Once understood, economics becomes part of the way we think about the world. If we don't understand it, many aspects of the way the world works continue to elude our vision and grasp.

It is striking how much of the knowledge of the Late Scholastics was lost over the centuries. Britain had remained something of an outpost in this area, due to language and geography, but the Continental tradition developed apace, in particular in France in the 18th and 19th centuries.

But it is especially striking that the major resurgence of Scholastic ideas came out of Austria in the late 19th century, a country that had avoided a revolutionary political or theological upheaval. If we look at Menger's own teachers, we find successors to the Scholastic tradition.

Mises wrote that economics is a new science and he was right about that, but the discipline is no less true for being so. Those who obstinately avoid its teaching are not only denying themselves a pipeline to truth, they are in active denial of reality, and this is no basis for recommending any way forward.

As for those modern economists who are stuck in the positivist-planning mode, they too have much to learn from the School of Salamanca, whose members would not have been fooled by the fallacies that dominate modern economic theory and policy today. If only our modern understanding could once again arrive at the high road paved for us more than 400 years ago. Just as the cathedrals of old retain their integrity, beauty, and stability, the Austrian School, as a descendent of the ideas of Salamanca, remains with us to speak an integrated truth, regardless of the intellectual fashions of our day.

CHAPTER 8

Economics
and Moral Courage*

I t must be really painful to be an economist of the mainstream today—at least, it should smart to some extent. In a financial and economic calamity of the current scale, people naturally want to know who issued the warnings about the real-estate bubble and its likely aftermath.

When private-sector jobs have not grown at all in ten years, and when ten years of domestic investment is systematically undone in the course of 18 months, when housing prices in some sections of the country collapse 80 percent, and when formerly prestigious banks go belly up or receive many billions in rescue aid, people want to know which economists saw this coming.

Perhaps it is these economists—the ones who had long issued the warnings, and not the ones relentlessly consulted by the media—who should be giving the guidance about going forward. Maybe they ought to be weighing in on whether the new stock-market boom is a reflection of reality, or another bubble developing within a bust that could lead to a secondary depression.

Among the mainstream, however, no one saw it coming. That is because they have never learned the lesson that Bastiat sought to teach, namely that we need to look beneath the surface, to the unseen dimensions

---

*July 26, 2012

of human action, in order to see the full economic reality. It is not enough just to stand back and look at points on a chart going up and down, smiling when things go up and frowning when things go down. That is the nihilism of an economic statistician who employs no theory, no notion of cause and effect, no understanding of the dynamics of human history.

So long as things were going up, everyone thought the economic system was healthy. It was the same in the late '20s. In fact, it has been the same throughout human history. It is no different today. The stock market is going up, so surely that is a sign of economic health. But people ought to reflect on the fact that the highest performing stock market in the world in 2007 belonged to Zimbabwe, which is now home to a spectacular economic collapse.

Because of this tendency to look at the surface rather than the underlying reality, the business-cycle theory has been a source of much confusion throughout economic history. To understand the theory requires looking beyond the data and into the core of the structure of production and its overall health. It requires abstract thinking about the relationship between capital and interest rates, money and investment, real and fake saving, and the economic impact of the central bank and the illusions it weaves. You can't get that information by watching numbers blow by at the bottom of your TV screen.

Then when the crisis hits, it comes as a complete surprise every time, and economists find themselves in the role of forging a plan to do something about the problem. This is when a crude form of Keynesianism comes into play. The government spends what money it has and prints what it doesn't have. Unemployed people are paid. Tricks to prop up failing industries abound. Generally, the approach is to gin up the public to engage in some form of exchange, in order to keep reality at bay.

Austrians counsel a different approach, one that takes account of underlying reality during the boom phase. They draw attention to the existence of the bubble before it pops, and once it goes away, the Austrians suggest that it does no good to blow another bubble or otherwise keep uneconomic production and plans going.

The Austrians in the late 1920s and early 1930s found themselves having to explain this again and again, but it was the onset of the age of positivism—the method that posits that only what you see on the surface really matters—so they had a very difficult time making points that were more sophisticated. They were like scientists trying to address a convention of witch doctors.

The same is true today. The Austrian account of economic depression requires thinking on more than one level to arrive at the truth, whereas economists these days are more likely to be looking for obvious explanations and even-more-obvious solutions, even when these neither explain nor solve anything.

This puts the Austrians in an interesting position within the intellectual culture of any time and place. They must go against the grain. They must say the things that others do not want to hear. They must be willing to be unpopular, socially and politically. I'm thinking here of people like Benjamin Anderson, Garet Garrett, Henry Hazlitt, and, on the Continent, L. Albert Hahn, F.A. Hayek, and, above all, Ludwig von Mises. They gave up career and fame to stick with the truth and say what had to be said.

Later in life, when speaking before a group of economics students, Hayek bared his soul about this problem of the moral choices economists must make. He said that it is very dangerous for an economist to seek fame and fortune and to work closely with political establishments, simply because, in his experience, the most important trait of a good economist is the courage to say the unpopular thing. If you value your position and privileges more than truth, you will say what people want to hear rather than what needs to be said.

This courage to say the unpopular thing marked the life of Ludwig von Mises. Today, his name resonates around the world. The tributes to him pour out on a monthly and weekly basis. His books remain massive sellers. He is the standard-bearer for science in the service of human freedom. Especially after Guido Hülsmann's biography of Mises appeared, the appreciation for his courage and nobility have grown.

But we must remember that it was not always so, and it did not have to be so. This kind of immortality is granted in no small measure because of the discrete moral choices he made in life. For if you had asked anyone about this man between 1925 and the late 1960s—the bulk of his career—the answer would have been that he was washed up, old school, too doctrinaire, intransigent, unwilling to engage the profession, attached to antique ideas, and his own worst enemy. They called him the "last knight of liberalism" as a way of conjuring up images of Don Quixote. When Yale University solicited opinions on whether it should publish *Human Action*, most people answered that this book should never see the light of day because its time was long past. It was thanks only to the intervention of Fritz Machlup and Henry Hazlitt that Yale bothered at all.

Mises was as undaunted then as he had been throughout his life, and as he remained until his death. He had made a moral choice not to give in to the prevailing winds.

Before going into that choice more, I would like to speak of another economist who was a contemporary of Mises's. His name was Hans Mayer. He was born in 1879, two years before Mises. He died in 1955.

While Mises worked at the Chamber of Commerce because he was denied a paid position at the University of Vienna, Mayer served as one of three full professors there, along with socialist Othmar Spann and Count Degenfeld-Schonburg.

Of Spann, Mises wrote that "he did not teach economics. Instead he preached National Socialism." Of the count, Mises wrote that he was "poorly versed in the problems of economics."

It was Mayer who was the truly formidable one. Yet he was no original thinker. Mises wrote that his "lectures were miserable, and his seminar was not much better." Mayer wrote only a handful of essays. But then, his main concern had nothing to do with theory and nothing to do with ideas. His focus was on academic power within the department and within the profession.

Now, people outside of academia may not understand what this means. But inside academia, people know all about it. There are people in every department who expend the bulk of their efforts on the pettiest form of professional advancement. What is at stake? Not that much. But as we know, the smaller the stakes, the more vicious the fight.

Among the prizes are better titles, higher salaries, the ability to get the best possible teaching times, to reduce one's teaching load (ideally to zero) and office hours, to advance one's favorite people, to get a larger office with a puffier chair, to know all the right people in the profession, and, best of all, to lord it over others: to be able to reduce the influence of your enemies and increase the influence of your friends in a way that can cause people to become your lifetime minions and supplicants.

With the state, there are even more prizes: to be close to politicians, to get outside gigs in which you serve as an expert in drafting legislation or in legal proceedings, to testify before Congress, to get called by the mainstream media to comment on national affairs, and the like. The point is not to advance ideas, but rather to advance oneself in a professional sense.

Outsiders imagine that university life is all about ideas. But insiders know that the real battles that take place within departments have very little to do with ideas or principles. Strange coalitions can develop, based entirely on the pettiest of issues. Professional ambitions are the driving force, not principles. There are people in every department who are highly accomplished, but whose accomplishments have nothing to do with science, teaching truth, or pursuing a vocation as a real scholar.

This has been the case for many centuries in academia, but it may be worse now than ever. These pursuits are often well rewarded in this life, while those who eschew them in favor of truth are pushed aside and relegated to a permanent low status. These are just some of the facts of life. This is what Hayek was referring to. And Mises's life illustrates the point perfectly.

But let's return to Professor Mayer. The main energies of Mayer were spent on an open war against his rival for power, Othmar Spann. This consumed him almost completely. He believed that he had to keep Spann at bay in order to advance himself. Mayer smeared Spann in every possible place and way, in a war to the knife. Note here that Mayer and Spann did not disagree on any matter of policy in any substantive way. It was all about position and power.

When he wasn't consumed with passionate hatred for and plots against Spann, Mayer spent the remainder of his energy building up his power base within the University of Vienna. It began well for him as the acknowledged successor to Friedrich von Wieser, who was the previous power broker. Mayer had established himself as the most groveling student of Wieser's. His reward was that Wieser named him as his successor, bypassing not only Mises but also the remarkable Joseph Schumpeter.

Then began Mayer's march. He called the shots. Mises himself was on the enemies list, of course. Mayer was in part responsible for denying Mises a full-time teaching position and salary. But that wasn't enough for him. He treated Mises's students very badly during examinations. For this reason, Mises even went so far as to suggest that his seminar participants decline to be officially registered, if only to prevent them from being harmed by Mayer. Mayer also worked to make it nearly impossible for any student in the department to write a dissertation under Mises. The politics were vicious and relentless.

What was Mises's attitude? He writes in his memoir, "I could not be bothered by all of these things." He just kept on doing his work. One can easily imagine scenes from this period. Mises is in his office writing and reading, trying to hammer out and perfect the theory of the business cycle or reflect on the problem of economic methodology. A student would come in to let him know about Mayer's latest antics. Mises would look up from his work, sigh with exasperation, and tell the student not to worry about it, and then go on with his work. He refused to be drawn in.

The Mises Circle was aghast by the goings-on, but the members did their best to make light of it all. They even made up a song, set to a traditional Viennese melody, called the "Mises-Mayer Debate" that featured the two economists talking past each other and sharing no common values at all.

At one point, Mises's circle grew into a full-blown economic society associated with the university. Mises could only be vice president, since Mayer would, of course, be president, since he was the master of the universe as far as economics in Vienna was concerned. And he never missed a chance to underscore who he was and what he could do.

Mises's position as vice president would not last. The time came when Nazism grew in influence in Austria. As an old-time liberal and a Jew, Mises knew that his time was limited. Sensing the possibility of even physical harm, Mises accepted a new position in Geneva and left for his new home in 1934. The society declined in membership and otherwise floundered.

In 1938, Austria was annexed to the German Third Reich. Mayer had a choice about what he would do. He could have stood by principle. But why would he do that? It would have meant sacrificing his self-interest for the greater good, and that is something that Mayer had never done. Quite the opposite: his entire academic career was about Mayer and Mayer alone.

So, to his ever-lasting disgrace, he wrote to all members of the Economic Society that all non-Aryans were hereby expelled. This meant, of course, that no Jews were allowed to continue their membership. He cited "the changed circumstances in German Austria, and in view of the respective laws now also applicable to this state."

So you can see, then, that all of Mayer's power over his underlings was bested by the greater power of the state, to which he was unfailingly loyal. He thrived before the Nazis. He thrived during the Nazi takeover. He helped the Nazis purge the Jews and the liberals from his department. Note that Mayer was no raging anti-Semite himself. His decision was a result of a series of discrete choices for position and power in the profession against truth and principle. For a time, this seemed harmless in some way. And then the moment of truth arrived and he played a role in the mass slaughter of ideas and those who held them.

Perhaps Mayer thought he had made the right choice. After all, he maintained his privileges and perks. And after the war, when the Communists came and took over the department, he thrived then too. He did all that an academic was supposed to do to get ahead, and achieved all the glory that an academic can achieve, regardless of the circumstances.

But consider the irony of all this power and glory. In the bigger picture of Continental economics in general, the Austrians were not highly regarded by the profession at large. Since the turn of the century, the German Historical School had captured the mantle of science. Their empirical orientation and stance against classical theory had, over the decades, melded nicely with the rise of positivism in the social sciences.

Never forget that the phrase Austrian School was coined not by the Austrians but by the German Historical School, and the phrase was used as a put-down, with overtones of a school mired in scholasticism and medieval deduction rather than real science. So our friend Mayer thought that he was master of the universe, when he was a very small fish in an even smaller pond.

He played the game and that was all he did. He thought he won, but history has rendered a different judgment.

He died in 1955. And then what happened? Justice finally arrived. He was instantly forgotten. Of all the students he had during his life, he had none after death. There were no Mayerians. Hayek reflected on the amazing development in an essay. He expected much to come out of the Wieser-Mayer school, but not much to come out of the Mises branch. He writes that the very opposite happened. Mayer's machine seemed promising, but it broke down completely, while Mises had no machine at all and he became the leader of a global colossus of ideas.

If we look at Mark Blaug's book *Who's Who in Economics*, a 1,300-page tome, there is an entry for Menger, Hayek, Böhm-Bawerk, and, of course, Ludwig von Mises. The entry calls Mises "the leading twentieth-century figure of the Austrian School" and credits him with contributions to methodology, price theory, business-cycle theory, monetary theory, socialist theory, and interventionism. There is no mention of the price he paid in life, no mention of his courageous moral choices, no mention of the grim reality of a life moving from country to country to stay ahead of the state. He ended up being known only for his triumphs, about which not even Mises was ever made aware during his own life.

And guess what? There is no entry at all in this same book for Hans Mayer. It is not that his status is reduced, not that he is noted and dismissed, not that he is put down as a minor thinker with enormous power. He is not called a Nazi collaborator or a Communist collaborator. Not at all. He isn't even mentioned. It is as if he never existed. Mayer's legacy vanished so fast after his death that he was forgotten only a few years later.

It is so bad for Mayer today that Wikipedia doesn't even have an entry for him. In fact, this talk has given more attention to him and his legacy than probably any other in 50 years. You might wait forever for another mention.

The Mayer line ended. But the Mises line was just beginning. He left for Geneva in 1934, accepting a dramatic pay cut. His fiancée followed and they were married, but not before he warned her that though he would write much about money, he would never have much of it.

And in Geneva he stayed for six years, having left his beloved Vienna and watched the world go through a shredding of civilization. The Nazis ransacked his old apartment in Vienna, and stole his books and papers. He lived a nomadic existence, unsure of where his next position would be. And this was the way he lived in the prime of his life: he was in his mid-50s and he was nearly homeless.

But as he dealt with the Mayer problem during those years in Vienna, Mises would not be distracted from his important work. For six years, he researched and wrote. The result was his magnum opus, a massive treatise on economics called *Nationalökonomie*. In 1940, he completed the book and it was published in a small print run. But how intense was the demand in 1940 for a book on the economics of freedom written in German? This was not destined to be a bestseller. He surely knew this while writing it. But he wrote it anyway.

Instead of book signings and celebrations, Mises faced another life-changing event that year. He received word from his Geneva sponsors that there was a problem. There were too many Jews taking refuge in Switzerland. He was told that he needed to find a new home. The United States was the new safe haven.

He began to write letters for positions in the United States, but think what this would mean. He was a German speaker. He had a reading knowledge of English, but he would need to learn it to the point that he could actually lecture in it. He had lost his notes and files and books. He didn't have any money. And he didn't know any powerful people in the United States.

There was a serious ideological problem in the United States too. The country was completely enthralled with Keynesian economics. The profession had turned. There were almost no free-market economists in the

United States, and no academic to champion his cause. There were a few leads he had on jobs, but they were only promises and there was no discussion of pay or any kind of security. He ended up having to leave with no assurances at all. He was almost 60.

But in the United States, Mises did have a major champion outside of academia. His name was Henry Hazlitt. Let me review Hazlitt's history here, too. He began his work as a financial journalist and book-review editor for New York papers. He became so well-known as a literary figure that he was hired as the literary editor for *The Nation* before the New Deal. His free-market views were not a special problem for him in those days. But after the Great Depression, liberal intellectuals had to make a choice: they had to adhere to free-market theory or embrace the industrial-planning state of FDR.

The Nation went with the New Deal. This was a major reversal for this organ of liberal opinion that had long championed freedom and condemned industrial statism. The New Deal was nothing if not the imposition of a fascist system of economics, but *The Nation* set a precedent for the American Left that this ideological tendency has followed ever since: all principles must eventually yield to the one overriding imperative of opposing capitalism, no matter what.

Hazlitt refused to go along with the change. He argued with his colleagues. He pointed out the fallacies of the National Industrial Recovery Act. He patiently tried to explain to them the absurdities of the New Deal. He wouldn't give in. They fired him.

H.L. Mencken saw the greatness of Hazlitt's work and hired him as his own successor at the *American Mercury* before turning over full control. Sadly, this didn't work out either, because the ownership of that publication did not like Hazlitt's Jewishness or free-market bent, and sent him packing yet again.

In different ways, in different sectors, and in different countries, it seemed like Mises and Hazlitt were living parallel lives. At each crossroad in life, they had both chosen the path of principle. They chose freedom even when it was at the expense of their own bank accounts and even though their choice brought professional decline and risked failure in the eyes of their colleagues.

Hazlitt moved to the *New York Times*, which back then did not have nearly the prestige it has today, however undeserved. He used his position to write about Mises's books like *Socialism*. This grabbed the attention of a handful of American business people like Lawrence Fertig, who later became

—like Hazlitt—a very generous donor to the Mises Institute. It was Fertig and his friends who knew of Mises's arrival in America, and they were thrilled. They had seen what a devastating blow FDR and Keynesianism were for free-market ideas. They put together a fund that would provide Mises a position at New York University, where he could teach and write. He was not paid by the university, where he was always a visiting professor, but through a private endowment.

Do you see how all of this links up? Hazlitt took the moral road, the courageous road, the road of sacrifice and principle. It was because of this that Mises, who had taken a similar road, could find safe haven in the United States. It was not the position that he deserved. He would be treated much worse than the Keynesians and Marxists. But it was something. It was an income to pay the bills. It was a chance to teach and write. He had the freedom to say what he wanted to say. That's all he needed.

So we see how these two men of principle, worlds apart, ended up being drawn to each other because they recognized a type: the man who is willing to do what is right regardless of the circumstances. Each could have gone another way. Mises might have been every bit as famous and powerful as Mayer had been, but he would have thrown away the immortality of his ideas in the process. Hazlitt could have been a high-status writer with a major outlet, but he would have had to surrender every ounce of integrity in order to do so.

Working together, they were able to overcome.

One of the people who had been drawn to Mises through Hazlitt's writing was the head of Yale University Press, Eugene Davidson, who had approached Mises about doing an English-language edition of his magnum opus from 1940. Mises had already dedicated six years to that book and it had sunk without a trace. Now he was being asked to translate it into English. It was a daunting task, but he agreed in principle. Yale then set out to find referees to approve such a huge publishing risk. Yale first went to Mises's old colleagues, and they were about as disappointing as referees as they were in other aspects of their careers. They wrote that there was no need to publish the book. Mises's ideas were old and superseded by Keynesian theory. But Yale persisted. Hazlitt finally managed to assemble a group of people who would endorse the book's translation, and Mises got to work again.

We all know the frustration that comes with losing a file on one's computer and having to recreate it. Imagine what it was like for Mises to lose a

1,000-page book, lose it to history in dark times, and to be asked to recreate it in another language.

But he was undaunted. He got to work, and the result appeared fully nine years later. The book was called *Human Action*. By academic standards, it was a best seller and remains so 60 years later.

Even so, Mises remained at his unpaid, unofficial position. He gathered around him students for his seminar, even though other professors warned the students not to take the class or attend the sessions. They discouraged their students from having much to do with him at all. The dean seconded their hostility. For Mises, who had navigated the wars at the University of Vienna, this was small potatoes, nothing to pay attention to at all.

Slowly his fame spread, but we need to remember that even at its height then in the United States, it was tiny compared with what it is today. In fact, Mises died a year before what is usually considered the Austrian revival, which is often dated from 1974 when Hayek received the Nobel Prize, a prize that was entirely unexpected and that had to be shared with a socialist—and that shocked a profession that had no interest in the ideas of either Mises or Hayek, whom they considered to be dinosaurs.

It is interesting to read Hayek's acceptance speech, which the Mises Institute published this year. It is a tribute to a profession to which he wanted closer ties. But it was not a loving presentation of the glories of academia. In fact, it was the opposite. He said that the most dangerous person on earth is an arrogant intellectual who lacks the humility necessary to see that society needs no masters and cannot be planned from the top down. An intellectual lacking humility can become a tyrant—and an accomplice in the destruction of civilization itself.

It was an amazing speech for a Nobel Prize winner to give, an implicit condemnation of a century of intellectual and social trends, and a real tribute to Mises, who had stuck by his principles and never given in to the academic trends of his time.

A similar story could be told about the life of Murray N. Rothbard, who might have become a major star in an Ivy League department but instead decided to follow the lead of Mises in economic science. He taught for many years at a tiny Brooklyn college instead, at very low pay. But as with Mises, this element of Rothbard's life is largely forgotten. After their deaths, people have forgotten all the trials and difficulties these men faced in life. And what did these men earn for all their commitments? They earned for their ideas a certain kind of immortality.

What are those ideas? They said that freedom works and freedom is right, that government does not work and that it is the source of great evil in the world. They proved these propositions with thousands of applications. They wrote these truths in scholarly treatises and popular articles. And history has vindicated them again and again.

We are living now through another period of economic planning and we are seeing economists split on both sides. The overwhelming majority is saying what the regime wants them to say. To depart too much from the prevailing ideology of power is more of a risk than most want to take. A small minority, the same group that warned of the bubble, is again warning that the stimulus is a fake. And they are going against the grain in saying so.

I'm with Hayek on this point. To be an economist with integrity means having to say things that people don't want to hear and especially to say things that the regime does not want to hear. It takes more than technical knowledge to be a good economist. It takes moral courage, and that is in even shorter supply than economic logic.

Just as Mises needed Fertig and Hazlitt, economists with moral courage need supporters and institutions to back them up and give them voice. We must all bear this burden. As Mises said, the only way to fight bad ideas is with good ones. And in the end, no one is safe if civilization is sweeping to destruction.

CHAPTER 9

The Misesian Vision*

I'm finding it ever more difficult to describe to people the kind of world that the Mises Institute would like to see, with the type of political order that Mises and the entire classical-liberal tradition believed would be most beneficial for mankind.

It would appear that the more liberty we lose, the less people are able to imagine how liberty might work. It's a fascinating thing to behold.

People can no longer imagine a world in which we could be secure without massive invasions of our privacy at every step, and even being strip searched before boarding airplanes, even though private institutions manage much greater security without any invasions of human rights.

People can no longer remember how a true free market in medical care would work, even though all the problems of the current system were created by government interventions in the first place.

People imagine that we need 700 military bases around the world and endless wars in the Middle East, for "security," though safe Switzerland doesn't.

People think it is insane to think of life without central banks, even though they are modern inventions that have destroyed currency after currency.

---

*January 25, 2010

Even meddlesome agencies like the Consumer Products Safety Commission or the Federal Trade Commission strike most people as absolutely essential, even though it is not they who catch the thieves and frauds, but private institutions.

The idea of privatizing roads or water supplies sounds outlandish, even though we have a long history of both.

People even wonder how anyone would be educated in the absence of public schools, as if markets themselves didn't create in America the world's most literate society in the 18th and 19th centuries.

This list could go on and on. But the problem is that the capacity to imagine freedom—the very source of life for civilization and humanity itself—is being eroded in our society and culture. The less freedom we have, the less people are able to imagine what freedom feels like, and therefore the less they are willing to fight for its restoration.

This has profoundly affected the political culture. We've lived through regime after regime, since at least the 1930s, in which the word "freedom" has been a rhetorical principle only, even as each new regime has taken away ever more freedom.

Now we have a president who doesn't even bother to pay lip service to the idea of freedom. In fact, I don't think that the idea has occurred to Obama at all. If the idea of freedom has occurred to him, he must have rejected it as dangerous, or unfair, or unequal, or irresponsible, or something along those lines.

To him, and to many Americans, the goal of government is to be an extension of the personal values of those in charge. I saw a speech in which Obama was making a pitch for national service—the ghastly idea that government should steal 2 years of every young person's life for slave labor and to inculcate loyalty to the leviathan—with no concerns about setting back a young person's professional and personal life.

How did Obama justify his support of this idea? He said that when he was a young man, he learned important values from his period of community service. It helped form him and shape him. It helped him understand the troubles of others and think outside his own narrow experience.

Well, I'm happy for him. But he chose that path voluntarily. It is a gigantic leap to go from personal experience to forcing a vicious national plan on the entire country. His presumption here is really taken from the playbook of the totalitarian state: the father-leader will guide his children-citizens in the paths of righteousness, so that they all will become god like the leader himself.

To me, Obama's comment illustrates one of two things. It could show that Obama is a potential dictator in the mold of Stalin, Hitler, and Mao, for the presumptions he puts on exhibit here are just as frightening as any imagined by the worst tyrants in human history. Or, more plausibly, it may be an illustration of Hannah Arendt's view that totalitarianism is merely an application of the principle of the "banality of evil."

With this phrase, Arendt meant to draw attention to how people misunderstand the origin and nature of evil regimes. Evil regimes are not always the products of fanatics, paranoids, and sociopaths, though, of course, power breeds fanaticism, paranoia, and sociopathology. Instead, the total state can be built by ordinary people who accept a wrong premise concerning the role of the state in society.

If the role of the state is to ferret out evil thoughts and bad ideas, it must necessarily become totalitarian. If the goal of the state is that all citizens must come to hold the same values as the great leader, whether economic, moral, or cultural, the state must necessarily become totalitarian. If the people are led to believe that scarce resources are best channeled in a direction that producers and consumers would not choose on their own, the result must necessarily be central planning.

On the face of it, many people today do not necessarily reject these premises. No longer is the idea of a state-planned society seen as frightening. What scares people more today is the prospect of a society without a plan, which is to say a society of freedom. But here is the key difference between authority in everyday life—such as that exercised by a parent or a teacher or a pastor or a boss—and the power of the state: the state's edicts are always and everywhere enforced at the point of a gun.

It is interesting how little we think about that reality—one virtually never hears that truth stated so plainly in a college classroom, for example—but it is the core reality. Everything done by the state is ultimately done by means of aggression, which is to say violence or the threat of violence against the innocent. The total state is really nothing but the continued extension of these statist means throughout every nook and cranny of economic and social life. Thus does the paranoia, megalomania, and fanaticism of the rulers become deadly dangerous to everyone.

It begins in a seemingly small error, a banality. But, with the state, what begins in banality ends in bloodshed.

Let me give another example of the banality of evil. Several decades ago, some crackpots had the idea that mankind's use of fossil fuels had a warming effect on the weather. Environmentalists were pretty fired up by the notion. So were many politicians. Economists were largely tongue-tied because they had long ago conceded that there are some public goods that the market can't handle; surely the weather is one of them.

Enough years go by, and what do you have? Politicians from all over the world—every last one of them a huckster of some sort, only pretending to represent his nation—gathering in a posh resort in Europe to tax the world and plan its weather down to precise temperatures half a century from now.

In the entire history of mankind, there has not been a more preposterous spectacle than this.

I don't know if it is tragedy or farce that the meeting on global warming came to an end with the politicians racing home to deal with snowstorms and record cold temperatures.

I draw attention to this absurdity to make a more general point. What seems to have escaped the current generation is the notion that was once called freedom.

Let me be clear on what I mean by freedom. I mean a social or political condition in which people exercise their own choices concerning what they do with their lives and property. People are permitted to trade and exchange goods and services without impediment or violent interference. They can associate or not associate with anyone of their own choosing. They can arrange their own lives and businesses. They can build, move, innovate, save, invest, and consume on terms that they themselves define.

What will be the results? We cannot predict them, any more than I can know when everyone in this room will wake up tomorrow morning, or what you will have for breakfast. Human choice works this way. There are as many patterns of human choice as there are humans who make choices.

The only real question we should ask is whether the results will be orderly—consistent with peace and prosperity—or chaotic, and thereby at war with human flourishing. The great burden born by the classical liberal tradition, stretching from medieval times to our own, is to make believable the otherwise improbable claim that liberty is the mother, not the daughter, of orderliness.

To be sure, that generation of Americans that seceded from British rule in the late-18th century took the imperative of liberty as a given. They had benefitted from centuries of intellectual work by true liberals who had demonstrated that government does nothing for society but divide and loot people in big and small ways. They had come to believe that the best way to rule a society is not to rule it at all, or, possibly, to rule it in only the most minimal way, with the people's consent.

Today, this social order sounds like chaos, not anything we dare try, lest we be overrun with terrorists and drug fiends, amidst massive social, economic, and cultural collapse. To me this is very interesting. It is the cultural condition that comes about in the absence of experience with freedom. More precisely, it comes about when people have no notion of the relationship between cause and effect in human affairs.

One might think that it would be enough for most people to log on to the World Wide Web, browse any major social-networking site or search engine, and gain direct experience with the results of human freedom. No government agency created Facebook and no government agency manages its day-to-day operation. It is the same with Google. Nor did a bureaucratic agency invent the miracle of the iPhone, or the utopian cornucopia of products available at the Wal-Mart down the street.

Meanwhile, look at what the state gives us: the Department of Motor Vehicles; the post office; spying on our emails and phone calls; full-body scans at the airport; restrictions on water use; the court system; wars; taxes; inflation; business regulations; public schools; Social Security; the CIA; and another ten thousand failed programs and bureaucracies, the reputations of which are no good no matter who you talk to.

Now, one might say, Oh sure, the free market gives us the dessert, but the government gives us the vegetables to keep us healthy. That view does not account for the horrific reality that more than 100 million people were slaughtered by the state in the 20th century alone, not including its wars.

This is only the most visible cost. As Frédéric Bastiat emphasized, the enormity of the costs of the state can only be discovered in considering its unseen costs: the inventions not brought to market, the businesses not opened, the people whose lives were cut short so that they could not enjoy their full potential, the wealth not used for productive purposes but rather taxed away, the capital accumulation through savings not undertaken because the currency was destroyed and the interest rate held near zero, among an infinitely expandable list of unknowns.

To understand these costs requires intellectual sophistication. To understand the more basic and immediate point, that markets work and the state does not, needs less sophistication but still requires some degree of understanding of cause and effect. If we lack this understanding, we go through life accepting whatever exists as a given. If there is wealth, there is wealth, and there is nothing else to know. If there is poverty, there is poverty, and we can know no more about it.

It was to address this deep ignorance that the discipline of economics was born in Spain and Italy—the homes of the first industrial revolutions—in the 14th and 15th centuries, and came to the heights of scientific exposition in the 16th century, to be expanded and elaborated upon in the 18th century in England and Germany, and in France in the 19th century, and finally to achieve its fullest presentation in Austria and America in the late-19th and 20th centuries.

And what did economics contribute to human sciences? What was the value that it added? It demonstrated the orderliness of the material world through a careful look at the operation of the price system and the forces that work to organize the production and distribution of scarce goods.

The main lesson of economics was taught again and again for centuries: government cannot improve on the results of human action achieved through voluntary trade and association. This was its contribution. This was its argument. This was its warning to every would-be social planner: your dreams of domination must be curbed.

In effect, this was a message of freedom, one that inspired revolution after revolution, each of which stemming from the conviction that humankind would be better off in the absence of rule than in its tyrannical presence. But consider what had to come before the real revolutions: there had to be this intellectual work that prepared the field of battle, the epic struggle that lasted centuries and continues to this day, between the nation-state and the market economy.

Make no mistake: it is this battle's outcome that is the most serious determinant in the establishment and preservation of freedom. The political order in which we live is but an extension of the capacities of our collective cultural imagination. Once we stop imagining freedom, it can vanish, and people won't even recognize that it is gone. Once it is gone, people can't imagine that they can or should get it back.

I'm reminded of the experience of an economist associated with the Mises Institute who was invited to Kazakhstan after the fall of the Soviet Union. He was to advise them on a transition to free markets. He talked to officials about privatization and stock markets and monetary reform. He suggested no regulations on business start-ups. The officials were fascinated.

They had become convinced of the general case for free enterprise. They understood that socialism meant that officials were poor too.

And yet, an objection was raised. If people are permitted to open businesses and factories anywhere, and we close state-run factories, how can the state properly plan where people are going to live? After all, people might be tempted to move to places where there are good-paying jobs and away from places where there are no jobs.

The economist listened to this point. He nodded his head that this is precisely what people will do. After some time, the government officials became more explicit. They said that they could not simply step aside and let people move anywhere they want to move. This would mean losing track of the population. It could cause overpopulation in some areas and desolation in others. If the state went along with this idea of free movement, it might as well shut down completely, for it would effectively be relinquishing any and all control over people.

And so, in the end, the officials rejected the idea. The entire economic reform movement foundered on the fear of letting people move—a freedom that most everyone in the United States takes for granted, and which hardly ever gives rise to objection.

Now, we might laugh about this, but consider the problem from the point of view of the state. The whole reason you are in office is control. You are there to manage society. What you really and truly fear is that by relinquishing control of people's movement, you are effectively turning the whole of society over to the wiles of the mob. All order is lost. All security is gone. People make terrible mistakes with their lives. They blame the government for failing to control them. And then what happens? The regime loses power.

In the end, this is what it always comes down to for the state: the preservation of its own power. Everything it does, it does to secure its power and to forestall the diminution of its power. I submit to you that everything else you hear, in the end, is a cover for that fundamental motive.

And yet, this power requires the cooperation of public culture. The rationales for power must convince the citizens. This is why the state must be alert to the status of public opinion. This is also why the state must always encourage fear among the population about what life would be like in the absence of the state.

The political philosopher who did more than anyone else to make this possible was not Marx nor Keynes nor Strauss nor Rousseau. It was the 17th-century philosopher Thomas Hobbes, who laid out a compelling vision of the nightmare of life in the absence of the state. He described such life as "solitary, poor, nasty, brutish, and short." The natural society, he wrote, was a society of conflict and strife, a place in which no one is safe.

He was writing during the English Civil War, and his message seemed believable. But, of course, the conflicts in his time were not the result of natural society, but rather of the control of leviathan itself. So his theory of causation was skewed by circumstance, akin to watching a shipwreck and concluding that the natural and universal state of man is drowning.

And yet today, Hobbesianism is the common element of both left and right. To be sure, the fears are different, stemming from different sets of political values. The Left warns us that if we don't have leviathan, our front yards will be flooded from rising oceans, big business moguls will rob us blind, the poor will starve, the masses will be ignorant, and everything we buy will blow up and kill us. The Right warns that in the absence of leviathan, society will collapse in cesspools of immorality lorded over by swarthy terrorists preaching a heretical religion.

The goal of both the Left and Right is that we make our political choices based on these fears. It doesn't matter so much which package of fear you choose; what matters is that you support a state that purports to keep your nightmare from becoming a reality.

Is there an alternative to fear? Here is where matters become a bit more difficult. We must begin again to imagine that freedom itself could work. In order to do this, we must learn economics. We must come to understand history better. We must study the sciences of human action to relearn what Juan de Mariana, John Locke, Thomas Jefferson, Thomas Paine, Frédéric Bastiat, Ludwig von Mises, F.A. Hayek, Henry Hazlitt, Murray N. Rothbard, and the entire liberal tradition understood.

What they knew is the great secret of the ages: society contains within itself the capacity for self-management, and there is nothing that government can do to improve on the results of the voluntary association, exchange, creativity, and choices of every member of the human family.

If you know this lesson, if you believe this lesson, you are part of the great liberal tradition. You are also a threat to the regime, not only the one we live under currently, but every regime all over the world, in every time and place. In fact, the greatest guarantor of liberty is an entire population that is a relentless and daily threat to the regime precisely because they embrace the dream of liberty.

The best and only place to start is with yourself. This is the only person that you can really control in the end. And by believing in freedom yourself, you might have made the biggest contribution to civilization you could possibly make. After that, never miss an opportunity to tell the truth. Sometimes, thinking the unthinkable, saying the unsayable, teaching the unteachable, is what makes the difference between bondage and sweet liberty.

The title of this talk is "the Misesian vision." This was the vision of Ludwig von Mises and Murray N. Rothbard. It is the vision of the Mises Institute. It is the vision of every dissident intellectual who dared to stand up to despotism, in every age.

I challenge you to enter into the great struggle of history, and make sure that your days on this earth count for something truly important. It is this struggle that defines our contribution to this world. Freedom is the greatest gift that you can give yourself and all of humanity.

CHAPTER 10

The Promise
of Human Action*

I n a 1949 memo circulated within Yale University Press, the publicity
department expressed astonishment at the rapid sales of Ludwig von
Mises's *Human Action*. How could such a dense tome, expensive by
the standards of the day, written by an economist without a prestigious
teaching position or any notable reputation at all in the United States, published against the advice of many on Yale's academic advisory board, sell
so quickly that a second and third printing would be necessary in only a
matter of months?

Imagine how shocked these same people would be to find that the first
edition, reissued 50 years later as the Scholar's Edition of Human Action,
would sell so quickly again.

How can we account for the continuing interest in this book? It is un-
questionably the single most important scientific treatise on human affairs
to appear in last century. But given the state of the social sciences, and
the timelessness of Mises's approach to economics, I believe it will have an
even greater impact on the present century. Indeed, it is increasingly clear
that this is a book for the ages.

Human Action appeared in the midst of ideological and political turmoil. The world war had only recently ended, and the United States was

---

*December 3, 2010

attempting to reshape the politics of Europe with a new experiment in global foreign aid. The Cold War was just beginning.

Virtually overnight, Russia went from ally to enemy—a shocking transition considering that nothing much had changed in Russia. It had been a prison camp since 1918 and its largest imperial advances in Europe had taken place with the full complicity of FDR. But in order to sustain wartime economic planning in the United States, and all the spending that entailed, it became necessary for the United States to find another foreign foe. By 1949, the United States began to fight socialism abroad by imposing it at home.

Indeed, on this day 50 years ago, the old idea of the liberal society was gone, seemingly forever. It was a relic of a distant age, and certainly not a model for a modern industrial society. The future was clear: the world would move toward government planning in all aspects of life and away from the anarchy of markets. As for the economic profession, the Keynesian School had not yet reached its height, but that was soon to come.

Socialist theory enthralled the profession to the extent that Mises and Hayek were thought to have lost the debate over whether socialism was economically possible. Labor unions had been delivered a setback with the Taft-Hartley Act, but it would be many years before the dramatic declines in membership would take place. In academia, a new generation was being raised to believe that FDR and World War II saved us from the Depression, and that there were no limits to what the state could do. Ruling the land was a regime characterized by regimentation in intellectual, social, and political life.

Human Action appeared in this setting not as polite suggestion that the world take another look at the merits of free enterprise. No, it was a seamless and uncompromising statement of theoretical purity that was completely at odds with the prevailing view. Even more than that, Mises dared to do what was completely unfashionable then and now, which is to build a complete system of thought from the ground up. Even Mises's former students were taken aback by the enormity of his argument and the purity of his stand. As Hans Hoppe has explained, some of the shock that greeted the book was due to its integration of the full range of philosophy, economic theory, and political analysis.

When you read *Human Action*, what you get is not a running commentary on the turmoil of the time, but rather a pristine theoretical argument that seems to rise above it all. To be sure, Mises addresses the enemies of freedom in these pages—and they happen to be the same enemies of freedom that surround us today. But much more remarkable is the way he was able to detach himself from the rough-and-tumble of daily events and write a book restating and advancing a pure science of economic logic, from the first page to the last. It contains not a word or phrase designed to appeal to the biases of the world around him. Instead, he sought to make a case that would transcend his generation.

To appreciate how difficult this is to do as a writer, it is useful to look back at essays we may have written last year or 10 years ago. Quite often, they have all the feel of their time. If any of us have written anything that can hold up 5 years later, much less 50, we should feel extremely happy at our accomplishment. And yet Mises sustained a 1,000-page book on politics and economics that doesn't feel dated in the least—or at least that was the consensus of the students we recently had in our offices to reread the entire work.

Consider Samuelson's *Economics*, which made its first appearance in 1948. It's no accident that it's in its 16th edition. It had to be continually updated to fix the theories and models that events rendered anachronistic in only a few years. Even as late as 1989, the book was predicting that the Soviets would surpass the Unitd States in production in a few years. Needless to say, that had to go. Last year, a publisher brought out the first edition—as a kind of museum piece, the way you might reproduce an old phonograph record. In any case, it didn't sell well.

Incidentally, when John Kenneth Galbraith reviewed *Human Action* in the *New York Times*, he called it a nice piece of intellectual nostalgia. Interesting. Does anyone read any of Galbraith's books today for any other reason? Our purpose in reissuing the first edition, on the other hand, was not nostalgia: it was to introduce a new generation to what it means to think clearly about the problems of social order. We still have so much to learn from Mises.

I think we need to reflect on what it required of Mises personally to write the book. He had been uprooted from his homeland, and much of his beloved Europe was in tatters. Well past midlife, Mises had to start over, with a new language and a new setting. It would have been so easy for him to look around at the world and conclude that freedom was doomed and that his life had been a waste.

Try to imagine the intellectual courage it required for him to sit down and write, as he did, an all-encompassing apologia for the old liberal cause, giving it a scientific foundation, battling it out with every enemy of freedom, and ending this huge treatise with a call for the entire world to change direction from its present course onto an entirely new one.

I'm sometimes accused of having an excessively pious devotion to the man Mises, but it is impossible not to notice, in the thicket of his dense argument, that he was also a singular character in the history of ideas, a man of uncommon vision and courage.

When we honor *Human Action* on this great anniversary of the book's publication, we must also honor the fighting spirit that led him to write it in the first place, and to see it through to its miraculous publication.

What are the political and economic trends that have come to pass in the last 50 years? The rise of new technologies, whose existence are best explained through a Misesian theory. The collapse of the Soviet Union and its client states, for the reasons explained in this book. The failure of the welfare state, again foretold in these pages. The widespread disappointment in the results of positivist methods in the social sciences, also addressed here.

Indeed, if we look at the failure of the welfare state, the persistence of the business cycle, the hyperinflation in Asia, the collapse of currencies in South America, the benefits we've derived from deregulation in our own country, and the meltdown of social-insurance schemes, we'll see that each is addressed and predicted in *Human Action*. Again, each is discussed in terms of timeless principles.

But none of these issues touch on what I find to be the most encouraging trend of our time: the decline in the moral and institutional status of the central state itself. Quite often in the press these days, pundits decry the rise of cynicism and antigovernment feeling among the public. But what does this really mean? Surely not that Misesian theory has come to capture the imagination of the masses. We are a long way from that. What they are decrying is the end of the old intellectual and political regime that was just coming into its own when Mises's book appeared in 1949, and has been breaking apart since at least 1989.

The same level of respect is not shown to leaders in Washington as it was in those years. Involvement in politics or the civil service is not valued as highly. In those days, the state got the best and brightest. These days, it gets those who have no other job prospects. The public sector is not the place to look for bandwidth. Moreover, hardly anyone believes that central planners are capable of miracles anymore, and the public tends to distrust those who claim otherwise. The political rhetoric of our time must account for the rise of markets and private initiative, and acknowledge the failure of the state.

Now, there are exceptions. There is the Bill Bradley campaign, which, as far as I can tell, is driven by the idea that Clinton has cut the government too much! And then there are the conservatives at the *Weekly Standard*. Last week's issue called for something new: what they have dubbed "One Nation Conservatism." The idea is to combine the conservative domestic statism of George W. with the conservative foreign-policy statism of John McCain. This is what might be called the politics of the worst of all worlds.

The entire approach fails to come to terms with a central insight of Mises's treatise: namely, that reality imposes limits on how expansive our vision of government can be. You can dream about the glories of a society without freedom all you want, but no matter how impressive the plans look on paper, they may not be achieved in the real world because economizing behavior requires, most fundamentally, private property, which is the institutional basis of civilization.

Government is the enemy of private property, and for that reason becomes the enemy of civilization when it attempts to perform anything but the most minimal functions. And even here, Mises says, if it were possible to permit individuals freedom from the state altogether, it should be done.

People were not ready for that message then but they are more ready for it now, because we live in times when government routinely confiscates one-half or more of the profits associated with entrepreneurship and labor. Politics consists of 100,000 pressure groups trying to get their hands on the loot. Why would anyone believe that it would be a good idea to expand this system?

Let me read you the rationale for this One-Nation Conservatism. It will inspire people to throw themselves into what they call public service. Public service has four main merits in their view: it "forces people to develop broader judgment, sacrifice for the greater good, hear the call of duty, and stand up for their beliefs."

These are all desirable traits. But I fail to see how they have anything to do with politics. Rather, a politicized society tends to produce the opposite: narrow judgment, selfishness, petty graft, and compromise. And that's putting the best-possible spin on it.

Who are the real visionaries today? They are software developers, communications entrepreneurs, freedom-minded intellectuals, homeschoolers, publishers who take risks, and businessmen of every variety who have mastered the art of serving the public through excellence—and doing it despite every obstacle that the state places in their way.

The real visionaries today are the people who continue to struggle to live normal lives—raising children, getting a good education, building healthy neighborhoods, producing beautiful art and music, innovating in the world of business—despite the attempt by the state to distort and destroy most of what is great and good in our world today.

One of the great rhetorical errors of Mises's time and ours has been to reverse the meaning of public and private service. As Murray Rothbard pointed out, private service implies that your behavior and your motivation is about helping no one but yourself. If you want an example, tour the halls of a random bureaucratic palace in DC.

Public service, on the other hand, implies a voluntary sacrifice of our own interests for the sake of others, and I suggest to you that this the most overlooked feature of a free society. Whether it is entrepreneurs serving their customers, parents serving their children, teachers serving their students, pastors serving the faithful, or intellectuals serving the cause of truth and wisdom, we find an authentic public ethic and a real broadness of judgement; it is in the voluntary nexus of human action where we find the call of duty being acted on. It is here we find people standing up for their beliefs. It is here we find true idealism.

It was Mises's firm conviction that ideas, and ideas alone, can bring about a change in the course of history. It is for this reason that he was able to complete his great book and live a heroic life despite every attempt to silence him.

The scholarly followers of Mises in our own time exhibit these traits, and inspire us every day with their innovative, principled, and radical approach to remaking the world of ideas. In their work for the *Quarterly Journal of Austrian Economics*, in their books, and in their teaching we see the ideals of Mises being fulfilled.

At a low point in his life, Mises wondered if he had become nothing but a historian of decline. But he quickly recalled his motto from Virgil: "Do not give in to evil, but proceed ever more boldly against it." With *Human Action*, Mises did just that. He was to die around the time that Nixon went off the gold standard and imposed wage and price controls, to Republican cheers. He didn't live to see what we see today—nothing short of the systematic unraveling of the statist enterprise of our century—but he did foresee that hope was not lost for the flourishing of human liberty. For that great virtue of hope, we must all be very grateful.

Let me also say how grateful I am to everyone involved in the production of the Scholar's Edition on this 50th anniversary, from our members to our faculty to our staff. Mises smiles today.

CHAPTER 11

Rothbard's Legacy[*]

Tributes to Murray N. Rothbard are often taken up with a listing his
accomplishments. This is because he was so astonishingly prolific
that there seem to be many scholars with that name.

As soon as you describe him as an economist, you recall that he wrote
some ten large volumes on history. But describe him as a historian and you
suddenly recall that he made large contributions to political philosophy.
But as soon as you begin talking about his libertarianism, you recall again
that he wrote vast amounts of technical economic theory.

It is the same with the venues in which he chose to write. If you look at
his scholarly-publications list, which is vast and expansive, you can easily
forget that he wrote constantly and for 50 years in popular periodicals of
every sort, commenting on politics, movies, culture, sports, and anything
else in the popular scene.

The problem grows worse when you consider the major parts of his
legacy. Let me list just a few:

- He was the economist who provided a bridge from Mises to the
  modern Austrian School, through his personal influence, articles,
  and especially through *Man, Economy, and State*, which appeared
  in 1962.

---

*June 8, 2010

- He developed the Misesian system in the areas of welfare economics, production theory, banking, and monopoly theory, and tied it all together with a theory of natural rights that drew on medieval and Enlightenment thought.

- He was the pioneer of libertarian theory who finally tied the principle of property rights to a consistent nonaggression principle of politics.

- He was the antiwar theorist who insisted that the cause of peace is inseparable from dream of prosperity.

- He rescued the 19th-century American hard-money school from obscurity and wove its contributions into modern banking theory.

- He demonstrated the libertarian origins of the American Revolution with the most extensive account ever of the tax strikes and prominence of libertarian theory during the colonial period.

- He explained the ideological upheaval that afflicted the American Right following World War II, showing the clear difference between the Old Right and the New based on the attitude toward war.

This of course only scratches the surface, but if I went on like this, I would use too many words and take up too much time, when what I would really like to discuss is Rothbard's methods as a researcher, writer, and scholar. I would also like to draw attention to his heroism.

A friend tells the story of a time when he was hanging around Rothbard's apartment one summer. The conference that was coming up that weekend was mentioned, and Rothbard had forgotten about it. Rothbard rushed to the typewriter and started writing. The words flowed from him as if the entire paper had already been written in his head.

The result was a 60-page paper on monetary history and theory, complete with bibliography and footnotes. The scene was recalled to me the way miracles are described in the Gospels. His jaw was on the floor in amazement.

The anecdote is inspiring but also intimidating for those who labor so hard to accomplish a tiny fraction of this level of productivity. We might look at what he did and become discouraged that we could never equal his productivity in even one small sector, much less take on all of his interests in so many areas of life.

Fortunately, we do not have to. The Rothbardian movement today is international. It is vast. It encompasses many sectors of life. He has inspired historians, legal theorists, philosophers, and economists. He is the muse of many bloggers, webmasters, editors, and essayists. He is the inspiration of many political activists, software programmers, filmmakers, and novelists. He is the model for teachers, pastors, investors, and even politicians. And this is as it ought to be. He set out to change the world. He left a legacy so that millions of people in all walks of life could take up the task.

It is natural to wonder what scholar today has inherited the mantle of Rothbard. To me this is the wrong way to look at it. Rothbard vastly broadened that mantle so that hundreds, thousands, and millions of people can wear it. What has replaced Rothbard is this vast network of ideas and those who champion them. This is how ideas are transmitted. They are not finite things that are transferred only from one brain to another and there it stops; instead, they spread and duplicate infinitely, landing in the hands of anyone who embraces them. The more compelling the idea, the more it spreads and the longer it lasts. This is the source of the power of the Rothbardian paradigm.

At the same time, we all do well to emulate this master when we go about our work. When Rothbard would take on a subject, his very first stop was not to sit in an easy chair and think off the top of his head; instead, he went to the literature and sought to master it. He read everything he could from all points of view. He sought to become as much an expert in the topic as the other experts in the field.

In other words, Rothbard's first step toward writing was to learn as much as possible. He never stopped taking this step for his entire life. There was never a point when he woke up feeling as if he knew all that he needed to know. No matter how much he wrote, he was always careful to read even more.

If you follow his model, you will not regard this as an arduous task, but rather a thrilling journey. A trip through the world of ideas is more exciting and exhilarating than the grandest excursion to the seven wonders of the world, more daring and adventurous than big-game hunting, and far more momentous than any moon shot.

There is another respect in which we can all emulate Murray. He was fearless in speaking the truth. He never let fear of colleagues, fear of the profession, fear of editors or political cultures, stand in the way of his desire to say what was true. This is why he turned to the Austrian tradition even though most economists at the time considered it a dead paradigm. This is why he embraced liberty, and worked to shore up its theoretical and practice rationale at a time when the rest of the academic world was going the other way.

This fearlessness, courage, and heroism applied even in his political analysis. He was an outspoken opponent of the US nuclear buildup and militarization during the Cold War. His opinion in that regard cost him many publication outlets. It cost him friends. It cost him financial supporters. It hurt his prospects for professional advancement. A surprising number of his articles were written for very small publications, simply because the larger ones were captives of special interests.

But time would eventually reveal that he took the right path. Forty years of pro–Cold War writing on the Right were made irrelevant by events. Rothbard's work during these years has stood the test of time. He is seen as one of the lone prophets of the collapse of socialism in Russia and Eastern Europe.

The choices he made in life were not designed to advance his career. They were made to advance liberty and truth. For many years, publications were closed to him. He did not teach in a prestigious institution. His income was small. Only very late in life did he begin to get his due as a thinker and teacher. But he never complained. He was grateful for any and every opportunity that came along to write and teach. His legacy is now a living part of the world of ideas. The people who tried to exclude him and write him out of history are mostly forgotten.

We call our program this week the Rothbard Graduate Seminar. The focus is on his great work *Man, Economy, and State*. In the Rothbardian tradition, the goal is to accomplish that most important first step toward making any contribution to the world of ideas: to open your mind to learn. Once the material is mastered, the next step is to do your own thinking and be fearless in embracing what is true.

I don't doubt that some in this room will extend some aspect of Rothbardian political economy at some point in your lives, perhaps even this summer. No one would be as happy about that as Rothbard. Murray loved his teachers. He loved books. More than anything else, he wanted to be a teacher and leave books for you to read, all toward the goal of changing the world. You pay him, and the cause of liberty, the highest compliment by doing just that.

CHAPTER 12

Hazlitt and Keynes: Opposite Callings*

J ohn Maynard Keynes was born in 1883 and died in 1946. Henry Hazlitt was born in 1894, eleven years after Keynes, and lived much longer, until 1993. Their lives and loyalties are a study in contrast, and mostly of choices born of internal conviction, in Hazlitt's case, or lack thereof, in Keynes's case.

Keynes became the most famous economist of the 20th century and the guru-crank whose work has inspired thousands of failed economic experiments and continues to inspire them today. He is the Svengali-like figure who implausibly convinced the world that saving is bad, inflation cures unemployment, investment can and should be socialized, consumers are fools whose interests should be dismissed, and capital can be made nonscarce by driving interest rates to zero—thereby turning the hard work of many hundreds of years by economists on its head.

Keynes had every privilege in life, and all the power and influence that an intellectual could have, and he used it all irresponsibly in service to the state.

Hazlitt was very nearly his foil. He did not come from privilege, did not enjoy a prestigious educational pedigree, and did not know any of the right

---

*February 7, 2011

people. He came from nowhere and worked his way up through sheer force of intellectual labor and moral determination.

Hazlitt eventually became one of the great public voices for free markets in the 20th century, writing in every popular venue he could and applying his enormous talents as a thinker and writer to defending and explaining free markets, showing how the classical economic wisdom was true and vastly improved by the Austrians, how sound money is essential for freedom, how market signaling works to achieve economic coordination, and how government policy is always and everywhere the enemy of freedom and prosperity.

Hazlitt's great book *Economics in One Lesson,* written the year that Keynes died, boils down all of economics to a single principle and applies it across the board to all the policies of government. It is crystal clear in its language and designed to be read by anyone, in an effort to achieve Mises's dream of bringing economic wisdom to every citizen.

Keynes's major work is *The General Theory* and it has been read by relatively few, mainly because it is so incomprehensible as to be nearly written in code. But then it wasn't designed for everyone. It was written for the elites by a member of the most elite class of intellectuals on the planet. Even more effectively, it was written with an eye to impressing the elites in the one way they can be impressed: a book so convoluted and contradictory that it calls forth not comprehension but ascent through intimidation. Its success is a remarkable story of the bamboozlement of an entire profession, followed by the misleading of the entire world. If there are still believers in what Murray Rothbard called the Whig theory of history—the idea that history is one long story of progress toward the truth—the success of *The General Theory* is the best case against it.

If I had to bet on which book will have greater longevity, however, I would go with Hazlitt. The same is true of Hazlitt's great legacy. He died without much fame. In fact, his days of fame were far behind him, arguably reaching their height when he was an editorial writer for the *New York Times*. When he was told that he needed to write in defense of Keynes's screwy plan for Bretton Woods, he balked and walked away. Thirteen years later, writing as a columnist for *Newsweek,* Hazlitt came out with a line-by-line refutation of Keynes's *General Theory*. It is arguably his great work, the one begging to be written. He alone had seen the need. It continues to teach us today, and serves as something of a manual for the errors of government.

Both Hazlitt and Keynes began their educations with an intense interest in literature and philosophy, but eventually settled on economics. Both were in a position to make a choice of theoretical paradigms given the intellectual and political content of their times. Both were major public intellectuals. Both considered themselves to be liberals in the way that term was used before the New Deal, meaning a general disposition toward favoring human rights, free trade, and open societies.

In this spirit, Keynes wrote in opposition to the Treaty of Versailles, which imposed savage terms on Germany after the war. He favored free trade and generally allied himself with that cause. Sadly, that tendency, which derived from the old world's love of liberty, was incompatible with his life's agenda, which he believed to be his birthright. That agenda was to rule the world through intellectual means by virtue of connections to the powerful. That essential humility that was at the core of the economics profession of the 19th century—the humility to embrace laissez-faire as a principle—was completely missing from his mind.

Keynes was born as a member of the ruling elite in Britain. His father, John Neville Keynes, and his father's good friend Alfred Marshall were very powerful figures at Cambridge University. They shepherded him and introduced him to the right people, and the time came when he was inducted into the secret, superelite society of top intellectuals in the English-speaking world. The group was called the "Apostles," and this was the group that would come to shape his ideas and his approach to life. The group had been formed in 1820 and included top members of the British ruling class. They met every Saturday evening without fail, and spent most of the rest of their time during the week with each other. Membership was for life.

It is impossible to overestimate the extraordinary intellectual arrogance of this group. They would refer to themselves as the only thing that is truly *real* in a Kantian sense, whereas the rest of the world was an illusion. Keynes as an undergraduate wrote to a fellow member as follows:

> Is it monomania—this colossal moral superiority that we feel?
> I get the feeling that most of the rest [of the world outside the
> Apostles] never see anything at all—too stupid or too wicked.

In the time of Keynes, according to those who have studied this carefully, the Apostles were dominated by an ethos that included two general traits: first, the bond that held the world together and would push it forward was the friendship and love that the Apostles had for each other, and that there were no other principles that really mattered; and, second, an intense disdain for religion and bourgeois values, institutions, ideas, and tastes.

It was in this period that Keynes met G.E. Moore, a philosopher at Trinity and Apostles member. His magnum opus was called *Principia Ethica*, published in 1903. It was a philosopher's attack on all fixed principles and a defense of immoralism. This was the book that changed Keynes's life completely. He called it "exciting, exhilarating, the beginning of a new renaissance, the opening of a new heaven on earth." It was this book that led him to believe that it was possible to completely reject morality, conventions, and all traditions. It might even be considered a kind of prototype of his later work.

These same values migrated to the famed Bloomsbury Group that Keynes joined after graduation. As many historians of the period have said, it was the most influential cultural and intellectual force in England in the 1910s and 1920s. The emphasis here was not on science but on art and the overthrow of Victorian standards in order to embrace the avant-garde. Keynes's contribution to their efforts was mainly financial, for he had made a fortune in speculation and spent lavishly on Bloomsbury causes. He also provided members with contacts in the world of finance and economics.

In discussing how immoralism and the rejection of principles applied to economics, Rothbard draws attention to Keynes's position on free trade. As a good Marshallian, he was a proponent during most of his early public life. Then suddenly in 1931, all that changed with a paper that loudly and aggressively called for protectionism and economic nationalism, a total reversal of what he had previously said. The press ridiculed him for his shift, but this never troubled Keynes, for as an Apostle and a champion of immoralism, he contended that there was no contradiction worthy of notice. He believed that he could take any position he wanted on an issue, and could live his life unhinged from any standards or rules. He was always ready to change his opinion given the new makeup of the political constellation and felt no burden to explain himself.

It was precisely because of this tendency to change his point of view on a dime that critics became tired of dealing with him. Hayek spent a great deal of time refuting him on various subjects, particularly Keynes's book on money, only to have Keynes dismiss the criticisms on grounds that he Keynes no longer held these views. He praised FDR and urged all governments to follow the New Deal. But when pressed on the details of programs such as the National Industrial Recovery Act, he would back away and grant that it was ill-conceived. His opportunism was palpable and infuriating.

As the Depression deepened, he began to see himself as the philosopher king of the world economics establishment, advising governments all over on their politics. His main target was the gold standard, which he regarded as a relic of a bygone era, the ultimate symbol of Victorianism, the monetary embodiment of morality and standards, a restraint on the ability of government to tinker with the economy, and therefore, from his point of view, the ultimate enemy of everything he hoped to accomplish. He had long ago written that "A preference for a tangible reserve currency is a relic of a time when governments were less trustworthy in these matters than they are now." What he meant, of course, was that with himself at the helm gold would not only be unnecessary but an impediment to the ambitions of economists.

Now we come to *The General Theory* that made its appearance in 1936. Let me introduce this book with a question. What would we call a person who believed that government policy can completely eliminate the scarcity of capital? Most all economists in history and even today would call this person a nut. The whole economic problem that economic theory grapples with concerns the invincible reality of the scarcity of capital. The idea that we can somehow concoct a system in which there would be no scarcity amounts to the belief that government can create a permanent utopia by pushing a few buttons. It is no different in kind from a belief in some kind of magical land of fantasy. It represents a fundamental failure to grapple with reality.

And yet this is precisely what Keynes hoped to achieve through his policy prescriptions in *The General Theory*. His idea was to create this land of universal happiness by

1. driving the interest rate to zero, and thereby

2. achieving his sought-after "euthanasia of the rentier class"—that is, the killing off of people who live on interest, and thereby,

3. eliminating what he considered to be the exploitative aspect of capitalism, that which rewards investors for their sacrifices.

As Keynes wrote, driving interest to zero would mean

> the euthanasia of the cumulative oppressive power of the capitalist to exploit the scarcity-value of capital. Interest today re-

wards no genuine sacrifice, any more than does the rent of land.
... [T]here are no intrinsic reasons for the scarcity of capital. An
intrinsic reason for such scarcity, in the sense of a genuine sacrifice which could only be called forth by the offer of a reward in
the shape of interest, would not exist, in the long run. ... I see,
therefore, the rentier aspect of capitalism as a transitional phase
which will disappear when it has done its work.

As you can see, Keynes was far more extreme in his views that the
media generally presents him. And the ghastly situation in which we find
ourselves today, where saving earns virtually nothing and the Fed holds
rates down to zero in perpetuity, seems to be the fulfillment of the worst of
the Keynesian dream.

As for the contribution of the book to theory, Rothbard writes that

The General Theory was not truly revolutionary at all but merely
old and oft-refuted mercantilist and inflationist fallacies dressed
up in shiny new garb, replete with newly constructed and largely
incomprehensible jargon.

Mises further pointed out that even Keynes's old and refuted ideas had
already had a good run of it:

Keynes' *General Theory* of 1936 did not inaugurate a new age
of economic policies; rather it marked the end of a period. The
policies which Keynes recommended were already then very
close to the time when their inevitable consequences would be
apparent and their continuation would be impossible.

What bad economic policies lacked was a prestigious economist to
come to their defense, and this is precisely the role that *The General Theory* played. Governments all over the world welcomed and celebrated the
book. As for the success of the book within economics itself, there are important sociological reasons to consider. Keynes's language was nearly impenetrable. He coined new terms on nearly every page. Rather than being a
disadvantage, this is often an advantage in a profession that has lost its way.

Keynes set out to divide the world into two broad classes of people:
stupid consumers whose behavior is determined by external force, and savers who are a drag on economic growth. The job of government policy is
to goad the first group into a different set of behaviors and pretty much
destroy the second group. Everything else in the Keynesian system follows from those two general propositions. This accounts for his hatred of
the gold standard, of traditional capitalism, and of the price system that

functions as a signaling mechanism for the production and allocation of resources.

It also accounts for why Keynes was one of the world's most passionate advocates of the rise of the fascist impulse in the 1930s. He celebrated the "enterprising spirit" of Sir Oswald Mosley, the founder of British fascism. He joined the *New York Times* in praising the central planning of Mussolini. Thus it was not a surprise when Keynes wrote a foreword to the German edition of his book in 1936, after the Nazis had come to power. He said that his book is more easily "adapted to the conditions of a totalitarian state" than to free competition and laissez-faire. Nor should it be surprising that Keynes also dabbled in anti-Semitism, praising even openly anti-Jewish tirades of Prime Minister Lloyd George and his brutal and public attack on the Jewish French finance minister Louis-Lucien Klotz.

A puzzling aspect of academia is how a sector that lives on its reputation for objectivity and love of science can be so easily bamboozled by charlatans, and the success of this book is a great case in point. Most economists over the age of 50 dismissed the book, but the younger ones regarded it as a kind of revelation that gave them a career advantage over their elders. Keynes's personal prestige had a lot to do with this.

As Rothbard wrote,

> It is safe to say that if Keynes had been an obscure economics teacher at a small, Midwestern American college, his work, in the unlikely event that it even found a publisher, would have been totally ignored.

But coming from a Cambridge don and student of Marshall, Keynes had huge advantages.

The Keynesian magnetism was so powerful that it even drew most of the former followers of F.A. Hayek, who was then teaching in London too. Most tragic of all was the conversion of Lord Robbins to the Keynesian cause. Robbins had written a great book on the Great Depression, one that the Mises Institute publishes to this day. It is written entirely in the Misesian spirit. But after having worked with Keynes on economic planning during the war, Robbins fell victim to his personal charisma, later writing of Keynes's "unearthly" brilliance and "godlike" personal stature. He wrote that Keynes "must be one of the most remarkable men that has ever lived." Robbins ended up repudiating his best work, only coming back to his senses late in life.

Hayek wrote many times that Keynes himself, before his death, was on the verge of repudiating what had become of the Keynesian system. This is based on Keynes's positive review of Hayek's *Road to Serfdom* as well as Keynes's own private words to Hayek himself.

In analyzing the evidence, Rothbard concludes that no such conversion was oncoming but rather that this was Keynes doing the Keynesian thing: shifting, moving, dodging, and changing, with no attachment to standards or principles or morality. He would believe anything and say anything and do anything to advance himself and put his class of technicians in charge of the world economy. It is remarkable that after a lifetime of writing, that his views would still be so difficult to pin down that even Hayek could believe, however briefly, that there was a modicum of sincerity in this man's words or actions.

Comparing his life and works to Henry Hazlitt's is like night and day. Hazlitt never held an academic position, had no family connections, and was never formally schooled in economics, but he was an extremely hard worker who read passionately and extensively, making an extraordinary career for himself, given that he was forced to drop out of school to support his widowed mother. He read in all his spare time: Mill, Aristotle, Nietzsche, Gibbon, and anyone else he could get his hands on, and kept extensive diaries of all his thoughts on their work. In all his studies, he presumed an old-fashioned view of his goal: to discover what is true, as a means to guiding his life and judgments.

All the while, he was also working. His first series of jobs followed in quick succession lasting only a few days. At each job, he would acquire a bit more knowledge than he had previously before getting fired for not have enough skills. Keep in mind that this was long before the minimum wage and other interventions. So his average salary grew a bit at each position: $5 per week, $8 per week, $10 and $12 per week. He finally worked his way up to become a reporter at the *Wall Street Journal*. He was paid 75 cents for every story, and he soon became invaluable to the staff.

It was in 1910 that he received his first real exposure to economics in Philip Wicksteed's great book *The Common Sense of Political Economy*. This is the book that would firmly embed him in a classical and marginalist perspective on economic issues and prevent him from ever falling away. He was also trying his skills as a writer. Sure enough, he managed to get his first book published at the age of 22: *Thinking as a Science*. The Mises Institute keeps this book in print and it remains one of the most inspirational and instructive books ever written on self-education and the obligation to learn.

He opens the book as follows:

> Every man knows there are evils in the world which need setting right. Every man has pretty definite ideas as to what these evils are. But to most men one in particular stands out vividly. To some, in fact, this stands out with such startling vividness that they lose sight of other evils, or look upon them as the natural consequences of their own particular evil-in-chief.... I, too, have a pet little evil, to which in more passionate moments I am apt to attribute all the others. This evil is the neglect of thinking. And when I say thinking I mean real thinking, independent thinking, hard thinking.

Here we have the tone and approach of a man with integrity, *intellectual* integrity, a man who is determined to find his way to what is true. The entire book reads this way. I'm particularly struck by his analysis of why some people attach themselves to error and will not let go. He might as well have been describing the seduction of the economics profession by Keynes.

In this passage, from this book he wrote at the age of 22, he is speaking of the prejudice that in particular affects intellectuals: their propensity to imitate the ideas that seem fashionable at the moment.

> We agree with others, we adopt the same opinions of the people around us, because we fear to disagree. We fear to differ with them in thought in the same way that we fear to differ with them in dress. In fact this parallel between style in thought and style in clothing seems to hold throughout. Just as we fear to look different from the people around us because we will be considered freakish, so we fear to think differently because we know we will be looked upon as weird.

He recalls a conversation he had with an intellectual in which he raised a point made by Herbert Spencer. The person recoiled and said that surely Spencer's ideas had been superseded. Hazlitt discovered that this person had never read Spencer and had absolutely no idea what Spencer actually believed about anything. Clearly Hazlitt, like most nonacademics, had a tendency to have higher expectations of the integrity of the intellectual classes than they merited then or now.

Nonetheless, he condemns the tendency to absorb prevailing ideas uncritically as completely foolhardy, as a pathway toward making life meaningless.

> I am willing to wager that most of these same people now so dithyrambic in their praise of James, Bergson, Eucken and Russell will twenty-five years hence be ashamed to mention those names, and will be devoting themselves solely to Post-neofuturism, or whatever else happens to be the passing fadosophy of the moment.

He goes on to speak what might have been the credo of his life.

> If this is the most prevalent form of prejudice it is also the most difficult to get rid of. This requires moral courage. It requires the rarest kind of moral courage. It requires just as much courage for a man to state and defend an idea opposed to the one in fashion as it would for a city man to dress coolly on a sweltering day, or for a young society woman to attend a smart affair in one of last year's gowns. The man who possesses this moral courage is blessed beyond kings, but he must pay the fearful price of ridicule or contempt.

After downtime during the war, he went back to work at the journal and resumed his reading, tracing footnotes to ever greater books. He followed the notes in a Benjamin Anderson book as the way to discover Mises's *Theory of Money and Credit*. He had fallen in love with economics in the same way that most of us did. He loved its elegance, explanatory power, its implicit love of liberty, and its central role in the rise of civilization. But it was not his only love. He read widely in literature and art as well, and found a market for his talents in this area. He moved from paper to paper until he eventually took at position as the literary editor at *The Nation*, which was then known as a liberal but not statist publication.

It was a high-prestige job for him, accepted at a period that would turn out to be a major turning point in our nation's history and also in his own life. In 1932, after FDR's election, the weekly would start to weigh on various aspects of New Deal policy. It was Hazlitt's internal constitution, that belief in truth, that led him to write in these pages what he believed about FDR's policy. He wrote about the real cause of the Great Depression, which he saw not as a failure of capitalism but as correction from a credit-fueled bubble. *The Nation* itself was not yet firmly entrenched as a propaganda paper for economic central planners, and so the editors let Hazlitt have his say.

He warned of the results of protectionism, price controls, subsidies, and economic planning in general. Not only would these methods not work to dig us out of Depression, he wrote, but they were contrary to the spirit of human liberty that liberals embrace as a matter of their creed. In saying these things, he was saying pretty much what any economist would have said a few decades earlier, but he also knew full well that he was going against the existing *Zietgeist* that Keynes himself was helping to craft.

Sure enough, Hazlitt won the debate but lost his job at *The Nation*. This was the first of many such events in his life, and it was something to which he would become accustomed. He had worked too hard for too long, and believed too much in the power of truth, to turn away from it. He had established a dictum early in life that he would not go along with an opinion simply because powerful and influential people around him held to it. He would have courage now and always.

It was not only his writing ability that attracted H.L. Mencken but also this quality of moral determination. Mencken named Hazlitt as his successor in what was the greatest American publication in those years, The *American Mercury*. He was there for three years until he moved to the position he held for the next ten years. He became the lead editorialist for the *New York Times*. There he wrote several editorials per day, plus book reviews for the Sunday paper. It was a stunning display of productivity. It was also probably the last time that the *New York Times* was correct on the issues of the day.

In 1946, this job came to an end in a dispute over the Bretton Woods monetary agreement. Hazlitt was relentless in attacking its fallacies and in predicting its defeat. The publisher came to him and explained that the paper could not continue to oppose what everyone else seemed to support. Hazlitt knew this routine rather well, and so he left without bitterness or acrimony. He simply packed up and walked away, and proceeded to write what would become the bestselling economics book of all time.

In these years, too, he had met Ludwig von Mises who had come to our shores in 1940. Hazlitt recognized in Mises one of those men with moral courage, a man who, as Hazlitt put it in his early book, is "blessed beyond kings" for his willingness to stick up for truth even at great personal cost. He used his position at the *Times* to alert readers to Mises's books and ideas. He helped Mises find a publisher for English translations of his books, and became a promoter and champion of the Misesian worldview. As we look back on it, it seems clear that Mises's life would have been very different without the help of Hazlitt. In some ways, Henry Hazlitt became a one-man Mises Institute.

But let's return to Hazlitt's succession of jobs. He went from *The Times* to *Newsweek*, where his "Business Tides" column educated a full generation or two in economic theory and policy, me along with them. These were remarkable columns, beautifully written and spot on topic every week. I'm pleased to announce that the Mises Institute is publishing all of these columns in a single volume this year. I'm expecting this book to help reestablish Hazlitt's rightful place in the intellectual history of the 20th century.

Now it was time for Hazlitt to take after the man whose ideas had dogged him for decades: John Maynard Keynes himself. Hazlitt was the first and still the only economist who has ever taken on the *General Theory* in a line-by-line analysis. He did this in a book published in 1959 which he called *The Failure of the "New Economics."* He writes in the introduction that he was warned not to do this, because Keynes's ideas were already unfashionable, but he decided to go ahead, based on an insight of Santayana that ideas aren't usually abandoned because they have been refuted; they are abandoned when they become unfashionable. And as far as Hazlitt could tell, there was no stepping away from the Keynesian fashionableness. And note too that this was written fully 52 years ago, and Keynes is fashionable all over again.

What Hazlitt discovered was that the book was much worse than he had imagined. He found no ideas in the book that were both true and original. He patiently goes through the book to explain what he means, taking Keynes apart piece by piece through 450 pages of thrilling analysis and prose, finishing up with a great concluding chapter that summarizes all the errors in the book.

I've not mentioned many of Hazlitt's other fantastic books, including his two books on monetary economics. On this matter, he was the perfect foil for Keynes. Whereas Keynes believed that the most important single step to destroying the laissez-faire of the old world was to demolish the gold standard, Hazlitt believed that there would never be a lasting regime of freedom restored without addressing the money problem. What Keynes wanted to destroy, Hazlitt wanted to restore and firmly entrench as part of the market order. They both agreed on the centrality of the issue in achieving their dreams, and in this they were both right.

But note where each ended up at the end of his life. Keynes died famous and rich and beloved, heralded by one and all for his brilliance. He was never asked to do anything courageous. He was never asked to make a sacrifice for what he believed. It would never have occurred to him to do so, for the very idea of a moral commitment or an intellectual responsibility was either unknown to him or totally rejected by him.

Hazlitt, in contrast, died at what was arguably a low point in his career. He had climbed to the top, but then was pushed back down again, eventually writing for and working with a small and largely embattled group of defenders of free enterprise.

We have in these two approaches contrasting images of the role of the public intellectual. Is this role to defend the freedom of the individual and to promote the development of civilization? Or is the goal to enrich oneself, get as close to power as possible, to become as famous and influential as one can be? It all comes down to one's moral commitments and personal integrity. In the end, this is the core issue, one that is arguably more important than economic theory.

Hazlitt made his choice and left us with great words of wisdom on the duty to support freedom.

> We have a duty to speak even more clearly and courageously, to work hard, and to keep fighting this battle while the strength is still in us…. Even those of us who have reached and passed our 70th birthdays cannot afford to rest on our oars and spend the rest of our lives dozing in the Florida sun. The times call for courage. The times call for hard work. But if the demands are high, it is because the stakes are even higher. They are nothing less than the future of liberty, which means the future of civilization.

CHAPTER 13

Hazlitt's Battle
with Bretton Woods*

A phrase we hear often now, and for good reason, is "the Austrians were right." The housing bubble and bust were called by the Austrians and, essentially, no one else. The Austrians were right about the dot com bubble and bust. The Austrians were right about the 1970s stagflation and the explosion in the price of gold after the gold window was closed.

You can tick through the issues and see that the Austrians have been right again and again throughout history: on price controls, on protectionism, on bailouts, on wars, on regulation, on prohibitions and civil liberties, and so on.

But issues concerning fiat money and the business cycle stand out because the Austrians possess unique insight. Only the Austrians have consistently warned that fiat money creates the wrong incentives for the banking industry, that central-bank manipulation of interest rates distorts the structure of production, that the combination of paper money and central banking leads to economic calamity.

These insights are not new, though many people are discovering them right now for the first time. From the moment Mises's 1912 book, *The Theory of Money and Credit*, made its appearance, and warned about the grave

---

*June 18, 2010

danger to free enterprise represented by paper money and central banking, the Austrians have been right.

That's 100 years of "we told you so."

Right in the middle of these years, there is a forgotten episode in monetary history that teaches us lessons today. It concerns the controversial role that Henry Hazlitt played in battling the Bretton Woods monetary system enacted after the Second World War.

Under Mises's influence, Hazlitt used his editorial position at the *New York Times* to warn against the plan, predicting correctly that it would lead to world inflation. For saying what he said, he was pushed out of his position at the *Times*. He paid a high price for being right, but this did not stop him. He kept going in his work of speaking truth to power.

The *Times* should offer an official apology and admit that their one-time editorialist was 100 percent correct. I'm not expecting that anytime soon.

Let us recount the events.

At the end of World war II, the monetary condition of all nations was deplorable. The Unites States faced a massive debt overhang from the war and yet this country was still a creditor nation to the world. The United States also had huge stockpiles of gold. Most everyone else was flat-out bankrupt, as only a gargantuan government program can accomplish. The main currencies had been wrecked and the main economies along with them.

As was the fashion, world elites assembled to plan some gigantic co-ordinated solution. They met from July 1 to July 22, 1944, at the Mount Washington Hotel in Bretton Woods, New Hampshire, and drafted the Articles of Agreement. It was nearly a year and a half later, in December 1945, that the agreement was ratified. On March 1947, one of the monstrosities created during event, the International Monetary Fund, began operations.

What was the goal of the plan? It was the same goal as at the founding of the Federal Reserve and the same goal that has guided every monetary plan in modern history. The stated idea was to promote economic growth, encourage macroeconomic stability, and, most absurdly, tame inflation. Of course, it did none of these things.

There are other analogies to the Fed. In the same way that the Fed was to serve as a lender of last resort, a provider of liquidity in times of instability, so too the Bretton Woods Agreement obligated all member nations to make their currencies available to be loaned to other countries to prevent temporary balance of payment problems.

There was to be no talk at all about what created these balance of payment problems. The assumption was that they were like bad weather or earthquakes or floods, just something that happens to countries from time to time. The unspoken truth was that monetary problems and related problems with balance of payment are created by bad policies: governments inflate, spend too much, run high debts, control their economies, impose trade protections, create gigantic welfare states, fight world wars, and otherwise undermine property rights.

As with all government plans, Bretton Woods was dealing with symptoms rather than causes and treating those symptoms in a way that enables and even encourages the disease. It pegged currencies at unrealistic levels, provided a bailout mechanism for governments and banking establishments to continue to do what they should not be doing, and thereby prolonged the problems and made them worse in the long run.

Governments have been throwing our good money after bad for a very long time. The plan, just as with the latest round of bailouts in the United States or Europe, was to dump money on near-bankrupt countries and thereby encourage them to continue with the very policies and practices that created the problem to begin with.

The core problem of the world monetary system after World War II was essentially that the gold standard had broken down, or rather, government had destroyed what remained of the old-fashioned gold standard through relentless inflation, debt, and devaluation. Economists in the Keynesian tradition had encouraged this, viewing money creation as some sort of panacea for all that ailed the world economy.

Keynes, the maestro of the Bretton Woods Conference, had recommended this and celebrated the results. To him, a flexible and standardless currency was the key to macroeconomic manipulation of his beloved aggregates. In a perverse way, he was right about this. A government on the gold standard is seriously constrained. It can't take a sledgehammer to aggregate supply and aggregate demand. It can't spend beyond its means. It must pay for the programs it creates through taxation, which means having to curb the appetite for welfare and warfare. There can be no such thing as a Keynesian state on the gold standard, any more then a cocaine addict or compulsive gambler can be on a strict budget.

Keynes's message at Bretton Woods, in Mises's summary, was that the world elites could turn stones into bread. And so under the influence of Keynes, the target at the Bretton Woods meeting was liberalism itself, which was widely assumed to have failed during the Great Depression. The elites also came out of World War II with a more profound appreciation for the role of central planning. They had reveled in it.

The Bretton Woods plan for monetary reconstruction did not go as far as Keynes would have liked. He proposed a full-scale world central bank and a single paper currency for all nations, which he wanted to be called the "bancor," so there could be no escaping inflation. That plan is still awaiting implementation. As it was, the Bretton Woods conferees, under pressure from the United States—which wanted the dollar to be the bancor—took a compromise position. They would create not a gold standard—though it was called that for reasons of credibility—but Instead a global gold dollar standard. Or, more precisely, a phony gold standard.

The Bretton Woods system established a gold dollar that was fixed at $35 per ounce. But it was the only currency so fixed. Every other currency could be a fiat currency based on the dollar. What this obligated the United States to do, as the main creditor nation to the world, was ship out dollars to the world while somehow maintaining the dollar's connection to gold. It was a prescription for disaster, as should be obvious.

To be sure, there is nothing wrong with having a gold standard in one country. The United States could do that now. But that was not what Bretton Woods established. The dollar was not convertible into gold at the domestic level. You could not go into your bank and exchange dollars for gold. It was only convertible on an international level, and only for governments, so that the United States was obligated to ship out gold instead of paper when it was so demanded.

This established some limit on credit expansion at home but not enough of one. Few were courageous enough to demand gold from the empire. Yet it is clear just from this description of the plan that the pressure to spend and redeem would eventually lead the United States to go back on its word. It took some twenty years, long after the original crafters of the deal had left the scene, but economic logic could not be gainsaid.

The breakdown really began soon after the plan was implemented. But most of the effects were disguised through currency controls. Once the 1960s came, and the expenses of LBJ's welfare-warfare state mounted, the Fed played its traditional role as the financier of big government. Pressure on the dollar mounted, foreign governments became more interested in the gold than the paper, and the whole cockamamie scheme unraveled under Nixon's welfare-warfare state. When the world entered the all-paper money regime, most economists said than the price of gold would fall from $35. The Austrians predicted the opposite.

From the very beginning, Henry Hazlitt saw it all coming and warned against Bretton Woods. He took the job of editorial writer for the *New York Times* in 1934, after having been drummed out of the editorial spot at the post-Mencken *American Mercury* because he was Jewish. Mencken had called Hazlitt "the only economist who can really write," and the *Times* job was a good position for him, one for which he was well prepared. He would write mostly unsigned editorials, speaking for the paper and not for himself.

In fact, when many years later his editorials were collected in a book edited by George Koether, called *From Bretton Woods to World Inflation*, his archives were the only place that revealed his authorship. Because he was writing them in an institutional voice, his tone was moderated to some extent, a fact he later regretted. Even so, anyone today has to stand in amazement when reading the *New York Times* editorializing against loose money, paper currency, central banking, and the like. But that was what Hazlitt accomplished.

He began his editorials in 1934 with a major call for the reinstitution of the gold standard. He urged that the United States and Britain jointly agree to a fixed gold standard. He said that this action would "symbolize a return to international collaboration in a world that has been drifting steadily toward a more and more intense nationalism." And truly, if one thinks about it, a world that had heeded Hazlitt's advise might have avoided the incredible calamity of World War II, the tens of millions of dead, the communization of Europe, and the bankruptcy and horrors the followed. And why? Because the nationalism about which he warned in 1934 would have abated, and all governments would have sought diplomatic rather than murderous solutions.

Of course, his advice was not heeded, and the drive to destroy money and prosperity continued, all the way to the globalized holocaust of World War II.

Now let us jump ahead, ten years after Hazlitt had written his first blast. Hazlitt was still advocating the same thing, not a system in which strong currencies subsidize bad policies, but a system in which each nation maintains the integrity of its own currency. That requires not centrally planned integration but the opposite. Instead of promising to intervene to bail out bad debt, nations should swear not to intervene. Only this path prevents moral hazard and maintains the gold standard.

He wrote as follows: "the belief that only a rich nation can afford a gold standard is a fallacy." Gold is suitable for every nation, he explained, provided it has something to sell. He concludes with these words before the Bretton Woods conferees gathered:

> The greatest single contribution the United States could make to world currency stability after the war is to announce its determination to stabilize its own currency. It will incidentally help us, of course, if other nations as well return to the gold standard. They will do it, however, only to the extent that they recognize that they are doing it not primarily as a favor to us but to themselves.

It is remarkable to realize that *these words appeared in a* New York Times *editorial*! We have here a world far removed from the Keynesian drivel of Paul Krugman. Put simply, there is no justice in this world when Hazlitt, who was correct, gets shoved out and his successors are of a school of thought that was completely wrong.

Keep in mind, too, that this was written one month before the opening of the conference. In the weeks that followed, Hazlitt was hot on the trail for news on what was coming. He seized on the statement of principles. It expressly permitted a change in the gold value of member currency on a unanimous vote from government.

Hazlitt spoke with a passion as follows:

> This is a provision which would permit world inflation. Experience has shown that it is extremely unlikely that any government will wish to raise the unit gold value of its currency.... The political pressures from time immemorial, and particularly in the last three decades, have been in the direction of devaluation and inflation.

Even before the delegates met, he correctly saw that the uniformity provision was not a limit to inflation but rather a license. If one country devalues, it sees the value of its currency fall on the international exchange. But if this is done in cooperation with everyone else, the country can avoid the penalty. This is precisely what accounts for the decades-old drive for international cooperation in monetary affairs. It is the same driving force behind why the Fed was concocted. So long as the system is decentralized, each bank or each country must deal with the fallout from its own bad policies. But if you centralize the system, bad policies can be more easily swept under the rug, with the costs widely dispersed throughout the system.

Or as Hazlitt wrote, "it would be difficult to think of a more serious threat to world stability and full production than the continual prospect of a uniform world inflation to which the politicians of every country would be so easily tempted."

Two days later, still before the conference opened, Hazlitt nailed it and explained precisely why Bretton Woods could not last. Under the plan, the creditor nations—meaning the United States and Britain—would pledge themselves to buy the currency of net debtor nations in order to keep the currency value at parity. Even if other countries devalued their currencies, the United States would be on the hook for buying it to maintain the fixed paper-to-gold ratio. This is precisely what led to the undoing of the entire system from 1969 to 1971. This, my friends, is prophetic.

Hazlitt was not just speaking for a sector of opinion here. So far as he could tell, and so far as anyone has been able to discern since these days, Hazlitt was completely alone in speaking these truths. No one else joined him, at least not in the United States. France had Jacques Rueff, who famously denounced the entire scheme. Switzerland had Michael Heilperin, who stood firm for the gold standard. Hayek in London actually submitted to the Bretton Woods delegates a draft plan for a real gold standard for every nation. It was completely ignored.

Only Hazlitt was on the front lines in the United States, by himself, writing constantly and passionately day by day to make a difference. More remarkable still, he was able to voice these lone opinions via the institutional voice of the *New York Times*. That was quite the accomplishment, a real testament to his own power to persuade.

All of his thoughts that I've so far reported were penned before the monetary conference had even met. He had already spotted the core problems of the proposed plan and explained how it would unravel.

On July 1, 1944, when the representatives first gathered, he greeted them with a punch in the nose. He questioned their competence, employing what would later be called the Hayekian knowledge problem. Here are his words from the editorial written the day the conference opened:

> it would be impossible to imagine a more difficult time for individual nations to decide at what level they can fix and stabilize their national currency unit. How could the representatives of France, of Holland, of Greece, of China, make any but the wildest guess at this moment of the point at which they could hope to stabilize?

The delegates must have read that passage and spewed their morning coffee across the table. Too bad that more of them didn't choke on their crumpets.

Hazlitt further said that the conference was planning to solve a problem by not realizing what the problem was. The issue, he said, is not a lack of currency value parity but rather the policies that are driving down the value of the currency in weak countries. He writes that it is of course possible to temporarily fix any price. But in the long term, it proves impossible.

He offers the analogy of a stock share that is worthless but nonetheless sells for $100 each. It is possible to maintain a high price, but when the resources of the buyer run out, the stock price will drop. There is no force on the planet that can keep a falling price from dropping once the resources to maintain it are gone.

Of course, this insight is a short summary of nearly all economic policy of our times. Whether the subject is houses, stocks, or wages, the goal of the stimulation packages has been to maintain high prices that cannot be maintained. As for the resources to make the high prices stick, in our day, the answer is to create ever more phony money to engage in this make-believe program.

In the midst of the Bretton Woods proceedings, Hazlitt hit the American delegates with another punch in the nose. He made fun of how the Americans, in particular, are under the impression that they can solve any problem in the world by setting up a machinery in the form of an organization. It could be an organization to make water run uphill or to keep rocks from falling, but the Americans are under the belief that if the president is behind anything, anything can be accomplished.

He states the contrary truth very bluntly. The restoration of peace and prosperity will not come from setting up another organization but rather by abandoning protectionism, capital export restrictions, important quotas, and competitive depreciation of currencies. America's greatest contribution, he wrote, would be to further balance its budget and halt deficit financing.

As for the American love of machinery, he writes that "genuine international economic cooperation after the war will be possible only if there is a profound change from the ideology of the Thirties."

As the proceedings dragged on, Hazlitt turned out to have foreshadowed the newest development. The delegates had not only planned to create the IMF but also create what was then the predecessor to the World Bank: the International Bank for Reconstruction and Development. The whole project, wrote Hazlitt, "rests on the assumption that nothing will be done right unless a grandiose formal intergovernmental institution is set up to do it. It assumes that nothing will be run well unless Governments run it."

Toughening his rhetoric, Hazlitt goes after Keynes by name, drawing attention to his preposterous claim that it would be *invidious* to discriminate between member nations based on their credit worthiness. Hilariously, Hazlitt sums up the plan for the World Bank with this general observation: "world economic revival will not necessarily flow from a plan under which taxpayers are saddled by their own Governments with losses from huge foreign loans made regardless of their soundness."

After the meetings closed, the debate on ratification began. Hazlitt made it clear what was really at stake: the freedom of the individual vs. the plans of government. "These agreements presuppose," he wrote, "a world in which the type of government controls developed in the Twenties and Thirties are to be expanded and systematized. What is contemplated is a world in which international trade is State-dominated."

Hazlitt must have felt intense pressure in these days. There are times in politics when the state and its paid experts make everyone feel as if some proposed plan is absolutely necessary for survival, and to be against it is tantamount to treason. In our own times, it was this way during the NAFTA debate, the WTO debate, and the debate on the creation of such bureaucratic monstrosities as the Department of Homeland Security and the Transportation Security Administration, or the drive for wars in the Middle East, or the hysteria for TARP et al. To be the outlier is to elicit heaps of scorn and derision.

It was the same with Bretton Woods during 1944 and 1945. No one ever found a logical problem or a factual error in what Hazlitt was writing. They didn't bother to. The point was that this was a mega priority for the international elite and no respectable paper could really oppose the plan.

As a way of showing that he was not a lone critic, Hazlitt began to write about other critics, who were very few in number. He seized on a small criticism offered by any journal or any association and highlighted it. But the critics were thinning, and every time one reared its head, he was summarily slapped down. All the while, the defenses of Bretton Woods were getting more extreme, with claims that if it didn't pass, the world would fall apart. The supporters were more and more open about their antimarket ideology, as when Secretary Morgenthau openly said that business can't run foreign exchange. It is up to the governments of the world to do it.

Hazlitt drew attention to these statements and also the open statements by Keynes that Bretton Woods amounted to the opposite of a gold standard. Hazlitt wrote his most poignant rhetoric in these days, claiming that the result of the monetary plans would be world inflation and massive economic instability. The internal pressures were increasing on him, as letters started arriving from London and DC to object to what the paper was saying. Hazlitt clearly saw the writing on the wall but still stuck to his guns all throughout the spring of 1945 as Congress was debating and preparing ratification.

Finally, the publisher of the *New York Times* had had enough. Arthur Sulzberger came to him and said, "When 43 governments sign an agreement, I don't see how the Times can any longer combat this."

Hazlitt began to pack his bags. After he left, his revenge was a massive article on the subject in the *American Scholar*, published later that year. Then he wrote the book that would become the biggest selling economics book of all time: *Economics in One Lesson*. His goal with this book was to propagate the core principles of economics, so that anyone could do what he had done, which was see the fallacies of the logic behind crazy government schemes. He wrote the book in record time and got it out the door as soon as possible. Of course it was a blockbuster. It remains to this day our bestseller book.

In 1967, Hazlitt also had a last laugh, if it is a laughing matter to see your worst predictions come true. Hazlitt was now a syndicated columnist with the *Los Angeles Times*. He wrote about the unraveling of the system, which finally happened in 1969. By 1971, the entire world was on a fiat-money paper standard and the result has been nothing short of catastrophic for societies and economies, which have been thrown into unrelenting chaos.

To be sure, Hazlitt was not, as he said, the "seventh son of the seventh son." He wasn't born with some amazing prophetic power. What Hazlitt did was read Mises and come to understand monetary economics. It sounds easy until you realize just how rare these talents were in his day and in ours.

There is another aspect to what Hazlitt did. He could have very easily relented or just stayed silent. It took moral courage and incredible intellectual stamina to tell the truth as he did when the whole world seemed to be against him. But so far as he was concerned, this was why he was put on the earth and why he got into writing in the first place: to tell the truth. He wasn't threatened with jail or violence. The only thing he had to fear was the derision of his colleagues. What truth teller in the history of the world hasn't faced that?

We might ask ourselves: why is it important to revisit this history now? As regards the details of Bretton Woods, it is extremely important to understand that this was not a genuine gold standard. It was a fake gold standard managed by an unworkable plan cobbled together by governments. It is the height of absurdity that supply-siders and others have for years been pining for a return to Bretton Woods and calling it a return to the gold standard. A new Bretton Woods would fail as surely as the first one did. It would certainly not be a step in the right direction to reinstitute Bretton Woods.

That Bretton Woods was called a gold standard was an exercise in obfuscation. It happened for the same reason that NAFTA was called free trade or the FTC is said to protect competition. The state has long used the language of liberalism and the market economy as a plow to push through its opposite. The gold standard was an early victim in this war over words.

A genuine gold standard is implemented currency by currency. It provides for domestic, on-demand convertibility. It allows for banks to fail on their own. It has no central banks. It surely has no international monetary institutions for lending bankrupt governments money. This is the only way toward real stability. Hazlitt said it in the *New York Times* and it remains true today.

If we want an impenetrable system of money and banking, we would follow Rothbard (Hazlitt once told me that the greatest achievement of the Mises Institute was to give Murray a "suitable platform.") and completely privatize the system, permitting private coinage of any money. This would be all the more viable in our own times, with digital payment systems and global communication. In fact, I'm quite sure that had the state not intervened, the internet would have already put together a competitive system of currency and banking that would exist completely outside the state's purview. A very viable means of reform we could undertake right now is for the state to simply do nothing. The dollar might be beyond salvation at this point, but money itself is not, of course. Money is an essential part of the market economy, so therefore let us let the market make it and manage it.

The stakes are impossible to overstate. Fiat paper money is destroying civilization right now. It has fueled the predator state. It has destabilized markets. It has wrecked balance sheets and distorted financial markets. It has wrecked the culture by leading the whole world to believe that prosperity can come as if by magic, that stones can be turned into bread. It might yet unleash a ravaging inflation that will be welcomed by dictators, despots, and cruel tyrants.

How important is sound money? The whole of civilization depends on it. We must accept no compromise. Down with government plans. Down with international commissions. Down with attempts to manipulate and control that always end in robbing us and making us poorer than we would otherwise be. We should embrace no more and no less than what the old liberals of the 18th and 19th centuries championed. All we ask is laissez-faire.

CHAPTER 14

Parallel Lives:
Liberty or Power?*

This is the tale of two economists who lived parallel lives, and then pursued two different and contrary goals. One was devoted to liberty and one was devoted to the state.

The first remained a teacher during his entire life, never in any prestigious institution and never exercising any power. Indeed, he used his post teaching *against* the exercise of power, and became the world's most powerful intellectual voice for radical liberalism or libertarianism. This man who loved liberty died in 1995 and his work has taken flight the world over. His books are selling as never before, all of them, and his star is rising by the day.

His name was Murray N. Rothbard.

The second one became the most powerful and influential economist in the world, practically running the world for a very long time. While in power, he was revered by everyone who was anyone. His every utterance could cause hundreds of billions to be made or lost in the market. But he will live out the rest of his days under a cloud of derision and discredit, defending himself against the perception that he created history's largest financial calamity.

His name is Alan Greenspan.

---

*July 9, 2010

Let us track these two lives and consider the choices they made.

As Charles Burris has pointed out, they were both born in New York City, in 1926. Rothbard was born on Tuesday, March 2. The following Saturday, March 6, Alan Greenspan was born. They had a similar background and upbringing, Greenspan of German-Jewish heritage and Rothbard of Russian-Jewish heritage. Both attended private schools and pursued their respective passions.

It is after high school their lives diverged. Whereas Rothbard followed a very mainstream path in academic economics—one that would seem to set him up as a giant in the profession—Greenspan went to the Julliard School of Music to pursue his true love, which was the clarinet.

As remarkable as it may seem today, Greenspan was not interested in economics or banking or any technical field. His interests were the arts, at least initially. There is nothing wrong with that, and indeed music has long been considered a foundation of a great education.

I mention this because it is an implausible beginning for the man who would later take the helm of the institution that would purport to manage the world reserve currency—a man after whom a professorship at New York University has been named.

Meanwhile, Rothbard chose to attend Columbia University. He was not an economics major. His passion was mathematics—and this was even before the full mathematicization of the profession. At Columbia, he studied under the famed statistician Harold Hotelling. It might have been Hotelling who led Rothbard to economic studies, but very early on, Rothbard the mathematician could see what was wrong with that application of statistical methods to economic theory. He would later build on Mises to construct a systematic theory of economics rooted in logical deduction in the manner of 19th-century theorists. All the while, his libertarianism was also in strong formation from early in his youth.

As implausible as it may seem today, Rothbard's biography would seem to be exactly that which would make for professional triumph with the mainstream of opinion and with the powers that be. What made that impossible were the choices he made—choices made on principle and for the love of truth and liberty.

Greenspan, for his part, declined to carry out his musical dreams. His grades were only average so he departed to play with the Henry Jerome Orchestra, playing saxophone or clarinet as necessary. He traveled the country on buses between engagements. Soon he tired of that life and in 1945 changed both his school and his major to economics.

The school was New York University, where Mises had begun teaching that very year. But Greenspan did not study with Mises, whom he might have regarded as a washed-up old man who could do nothing for his primary concern, which was his career. Instead, he chose the division called "the factory": 9,000 students competed in various fields of specialization in business. He graduated with honors in 1948 and enrolled in the masters program, graduating in 1950.

At this point, the lives of Rothbard and Greenspan briefly intersect in an interesting way: at Columbia University. Two years earlier, Rothbard had received his own masters in economics from Columbia, and had enrolled in the PhD program. Professor Arthur Burns was the most prominent faculty member. Burns would later become Eisenhower's head of the Council of Economic Advisers and head of the Federal Reserve. One might say that he was the Greenspan of his day.

Greenspan dropped out of the Columbia economics program to follow Burns to Washington and model himself after his tendency toward chasing powerful positions and powerful people. Greenspan watched Burns carefully, very impressed at how economics in an age of positivism can be used in the service of state-connected careers.

Rothbard meanwhile stayed behind at Columbia, writing and studying. One of his seminal articles in this period was published in a book in honor of Mises—that supposedly washed-up old man who just so happened to have a penchant for speaking truth to power.

Just as Burns became Greenspan's model, Mises had become Rothbard's model. Two more opposing career paths can hardly be imagined. Mises had been tossed out of two countries for his principled stance, and even forfeited a prestigious position in the profession for being unwilling to go along with the Keynesian revolution.

Rothbard would follow a similar path. His article written in honor of Mises, published in 1956, was a reconstruction of utility and welfare economics along nonmathematical lines.

Here we have the graduate student doing what a principled person does: he was pursuing truth through research and writing. He might have chosen to echo the rising Keynesianism and positivism of his day. Certainly he was intellectually capable of become the master of both fields. Instead, he rejected them intellectually and took a different path along lines laid out by Mises.

And what was Greenspan doing? He was running around Washington pandering to the big shots, watching their every move, striving to be like them, and attempting to follow in their footsteps by cultivating press contacts and relationships to people in high places.

Rothbard received his PhD in 1956 but only after jumping over a thousand barriers that had been put in his path by none other than Greenspan's own mentor. There were times when Burns's recalcitrance drove Murray to despair. He felt that he could not comply with Burns's dictates and could not please Burns—and that Burns seemed to be sabotaging his work.

Ironically, Rothbard and Burns had known each other since childhood. They lived in the same apartment building since high school. There can be no question that this was a personal attack against Murray.

Only once Burns became so wrapped up in Washington politics that he could no longer care did Rothbard finally win out. His PhD was awarded in 1956.

Now let me make a few comments about Rothbard's dissertation. It was an empirical account of America's first serious business cycle, the panic of 1819. He scoured every source he could, producing many pages of detailed economic data. He also knew the importance of ideology and personality in the history of economics, so he recounted the debates over the policy response. Then as now, people urged intervention. But unlike today, the government did not respond to the demands for inflation, price supports, bailouts, and fiscal stimulus. As a result, the panic ended and the economy recovered very quickly.

What was the fate of this dissertation? For more than 50 years, it has been the standard reference on this episode. It was printed and reprinted many times. Today, the Mises Institute has an edition out of this book and it continues to sell on a large scale.

Let me hop ahead to Greenspan's dissertation, which wasn't filed with New York University until two decades later, in 1977. It was quickly sealed and continues to be unavailable to anyone. No one had any idea what was in it until last year, when a single copy was leaked to a reporter for *Barron's*. What it contained was so irrelevant that it barely made the news. It was a collection of reports he had written for various purposes over the previous 20 years—a PhD granted for life experience, as it were.

What did Greenspan do in the intervening years? He founded a consulting company, Townsend-Greenspan and worked for the National Industrial Conference Board.

To understand Greenspan's firm and what it did, it is important to understand the role of the economic expert in an age of positivism. In the postwar period, the scientist with Gnostic-style knowledge and shadowy connections to power ascended to massive public fame. The substance itself didn't matter so much as the illusion of expertise. What his firm sold was Greenspan—to such powerful, regime clients as J.P. Morgan and Co.

Greenspan carefully crafted his image as an omniscient pundit on all matters related to economics. He used his connections to Burns and rising connections to all related power elites to build up a reputation as a monk-like data collector, pouring over charts and coming up with printable comments and predictions.

It was mostly illusion. There were no charts and data collections and machines to make perfect predictions. What Greenspan did was commodify his own pandering ways and sell them to a culture hungry for illusions.

All throughout the 1960s and the decades following, he worked to craft his persona to fit perfectly with the prevailing ethos. That ethos was statism—the glorification of central management by the experts. Greenspan sought to be top of the heap.

Let me say a few words about Greenspan's connection to Ayn Rand. The press routinely misunderstands the meaning of this relationship. The only writer who I think has gotten it right, aside from people in the inner circle like George Reisman and Nathaniel Branden, is Frederick Sheehan, author of *Panderer to Power*. Sheehan points out that Greenspan's relationship to the Rand circle was always opportunistic and never really had any effect on Greenspan's life.

She was a famous author on the rise. Greenspan was a master of hitching his wagon to any horse on the move. Rand herself called him the "undertaker." She would frequently ask her associates, "Do you think Alan might basically be a social climber?" Her intuition was, of course, correct.

But what the Rand episode further illustrates is actually terribly unflattering for Greenspan. It is bad enough for a person to cravenly seek power while remaining in ignorance. But as Greenspan revealed in his 1966 article called "Gold and Economic Freedom," he actually knew the truth. He knew that the Fed creates business cycles—he wrote this in his article, even getting the story of the Great Depression right. He knew that fiat money builds the state. He said that gold is the only monetary guarantee of freedom.

It is bad enough when a person devotes his life to the service of power when he does it in a state of intellectual ignorance. But when the same person pursues this path in a state of published knowledge, it is nothing short of reprehensible. Thus was his relationship to Rand no different from his relationship to anyone else: he used her as a steppingstone toward his real goal.

It was only a few years following this article that Greenspan angled his way into the Nixon campaign of 1968, taking the job of coordinator of domestic-policy research. He began a shuttle back and forth between New York and Washington that would define the rest of his life.

In 1970, his mentor Burns was sworn in as the head of the Fed—and here is when Greenspan set his sights on that position as his lifetime goal. Every choice he made after that point was dedicated to this. All the while, he maintained his high public profile, making as many as 80 speeches a year and pulling in huge consulting fees, while otherwise pretending to live a monastic existence, studying charts and tables and doling out bits of advise and wisdom for high dollars.

Despite the personality cult he was building, his predictions were almost always wrong. Let me give only the most famous example. On January 7, 1973, the *New York Times* featured his picture with a spread on brilliant market forecasters. He was quoted as follows: "It's very rare that you can be as unqualifiedly bullish as you can now." Four days later, the market peaked and bottomed out 46 percent lower one year later. This was typical for him: somehow able to build a reputation as a prophet while being wrong on everything. His method was always the same: using high-flown rhetoric and obscure language while dissembling and faking his way through life.

It was a perfect method for government work. And so, that same year, he became head of the Council of Economic Advisers. In 1974, he urged President Ford to propose a new tax as a means of combating inflation. He was involved in the "Whip Inflation Now" campaign, complete with WIN buttons—though he knew full well that the real culprit was not a lack of morale but a Fed that would not stop the printing press.

A few years later he wormed his way into the Reagan inner circle and became head of the Social Security Commission that ended up raising payroll taxes, which seemed to save the system but only ended up delaying the inevitable.

All of this was mere prelude toward 1987, when the goal of his career was at hand. He was nominated for the position he had been training for during his entire life: head of the Fed. What happened soon after was the famous stock market crash of 1987. Here he did what he would do again and again during his 20-year tenure. He met every crisis with the same tactic: he opened the monetary spigots.

Monetary pumping was his one weapon. Think of the occasions: the Mexican debt crisis of 1996, the Asian Contagion of 1997, Long-Term Capital Management in 1998, the Y2K crisis of 1999 and 2000, the dot-com collapse, and finally the 9-11 terrorist incidents in Washington and New York. Oh, and never forget that Greenspan, on November 13, 2001, received the Enron Prize.

What was behind all of this? Essentially, he proved himself adept at serving the state whenever it needed help. Politicians used Greenspan as what Sheehan calls their "air-raid shelter." He did them a favor and they returned it by appointing him again and again, and they fawned over him as no one has ever been fawned over. And it's no wonder. He was history's biggest counterfeiter.

You can see the map of this in the federal-funds rate. Looking at the chart from the 1960s to the present, we see a huge arch, with the peak in 1979, and the rate trending steadily downward to the present level of zero. The only way this could be justified would be through a large increase in savings and capital, and we have not seen this. This picture of lower and lower rates is wholly artificial. Not only that, they are bubble inducing in the extreme.

What we are experiencing now, in the United States and other countries, is a direct result of Greenspan's tenure, which led to the greatest financial catastrophe in modern times. And make no mistake: every bit of this can be blamed on Greenspan directly.

We know from on-record reports of everyone who worked with him that he ruled the Federal Open Market Committee meetings with an iron fist, never seeking anyone else's opinion nor tolerating dissent to his political intuitions. He would beat back any contrary view with withering stares and implicit and explicit rebukes. It was rule by fear and intimidation. He would frequently make declarations on the state of the economy that had no basis at all in reality, and everyone in the room would know it. But after a while, it became clear that no one could penetrate his brain. Instead, those gathered would just roll their eyes and walk away in despair, muttering among themselves. He could make or break subordinates and colleagues.

He continued to cultivate his public image as a way of crushing disagreement within the Fed. The message he sent through his high status was this: don't you dare disagree with this god on earth whom all people adore. For a time, we had the entire Wall Street and Washington establishment singing one long and united chorus of the hymn Thank God for Greenspan. He encouraged this, sending his minions out to tell the press that he deserved credit for all things: an uptick in employment, a downtick in the trade deficit, an optimistic earnings report from Wall Street. No matter what the news, he would take credit for it, even if the news had no bearing at all on any Fed policies.

Those were crazy times. A fake article appeared in the *New Republic* that told of a cult on Wall Street involving candles and an iconic image of Greenspan in the back room. The story was preposterous but believable. It took a very long time before anyone figured out that it was a fake.

As for his behavior within the Fed itself, his war on dissent, typical of any dictator, was too much for anyone at the Fed with intelligence and integrity. Janet Yellen resigned as governor in 1997, saying bitterly as she left that it is a "great job, if you like to travel around the country and read speeches written by the staff." She recalled, for example, that Greenspan would not even let her talk to the Fed staff because he feared that they would develop some affection or loyalty toward anyone but Greenspan personally.

Bert Ely, a Fed consultant, concludes with a point written about most despots in human history: "The chairman is not a secure man. He has to be one in the spotlight, and he doesn't want competition."

I don't need to tell you how the story of Greenspan ends. His world came crashing down around him. He spends all of his time today trying to explain his way out of the blame. Much to his everlasting disgrace, he has intimated on many occasions that the meltdown of 2008 was not his failure or a failure of the government at all but a result of inherent flaws in the market.

Ayn Rand speculated that this undertaker might just be a social climber. She did not and could not have known that he would eventually climb his way to the top, fall all the way down, and while he was writhing in pain would betray the entire cause to which he pretended devotion. But anyone who looked at his life could see the pattern. It was not a complex one. He served the state. As Rothbard himself wrote of Greenspan, "Greenspan's real qualification is that he can be trusted never to rock the establishment's boat." Indeed he served the establishment from the first day to the last.

Now, I would like to turn back to Rothbard and his life. When we last left him, he had completed his dissertation. He was about to embark on an enormous journey that would consume his entire life. He published in the established journals as long as he could but at some point, his quest for truth and love of liberty meant that he would be cut off from them.

Despite his brilliance, background, and credentials, he did not get a prestigious academic post. He worked for a private academic foundation, reviewing all the latest books on history, philosophy, law, and economics. His massive treatise on economics that appeared in 1962 began as a tutorial written on behalf of this foundation.

When he did get a position, it was at Brooklyn Polytechnic in New York. He had a dumpy office and taught mostly unimpressive students. But it hardly mattered at all to him. He had the freedom to write and publish and tell the truth, and that's what he wanted more than anything.

And yet even here, his options were limited. One might think that, as a supporter of the free market, conservative journals of opinion would be open to him. But soon after the Cold War intensified, he could no longer be quiet on an issue that was vastly important to him, namely, the relationship between liberty and military expansionism. He saw the warfare state as nothing but a species of socialism. And so he adhered to the credo of the old classical liberals: a free market plus a peaceful international outlook. For this, he was excommunicated by the conservatives.

The result was that he ended up building his own global movement, one that began in his living room and extended to the whole human race. His two-dozen books and thousands of articles ended up inspiring a vast, worldwide movement for liberty. His economic writings bridged the gap between Mises and the current generation of Austrians. His wonderful personality demonstrated to one and all that it is possible to have fun while fighting leviathan.

As for Rothbard's own character, the contrast with Greenspan could not be starker. If Greenspan was the dreary undertaker, Rothbard was the happy warrior. Rothbard thrilled to spend time with students and faculty and anyone interested in liberty. When you spoke to him, he was glad to talk about the field of interest that was the other person's specialization. Whether it was history, philosophy, ethics, economics, politics, religion, Renaissance painting, music, sports, Baroque church architecture, or even the soaps on TV, he always made others feel more important.

He was always excited to give credit to others and to draw attention to the contribution of everyone to the great cause. He never held a grudge for long: even for those who betrayed him personally, there was always an opportunity for reconciliation open. All of these traits extended from his amazing generosity of spirit, which I attribute to his love of truth above all else.

His too-short life was cut off in 1995. But that was also the year that the web browser became common in offices and homes. Those classes that Rothbard taught in his small New York classroom are now being broadcast around the world through iTunes and Mises.org. His books are all in print and selling as never before. There are not only his books but books on his books and an entire literature growing up around his legacy.

Many have said that Rothbard was his own worst enemy. People said the same of Mises. The idea here is that they could have helped their careers by going along to get along. That is true enough. But is getting along all we really want out of life? Or do we want to make a difference in a way that will outlast us?

At some point in all our lives, we will all come to realize that all the money and all the power and goods we can accumulate will be useless to us after we die. Even large fortunes can dissipate after a generation or two. The legacy we will leave on this earth comes down to the principles by which we lived. It is the ideas we hold and the way we pursued them that is the source of our immortality.

Greenspan will leave an economy in shambles and a lifetime of pandering. Rothbard left a grand vision of liberty united with science, an example of what it means to truly think long term.

In all ages and in all times, people must make a choice. Will we accept the world as it is and try to fit in, getting as much as we can from the system until we bow out? Or will we stick to principle, pay whatever price that involves, and leave the world a better place? I submit to you that anyone who has ever truly loved liberty has chosen the second course. That is the course that the Mises Institute is dedicated to following. May we each make that choice too.

CHAPTER 15

Liberty's Benefactor*

In every age, the idea of liberty needs benefactors, far-seeing people willing to make personal sacrifices so that each new generation is taught
not to take freedom for granted, but rather to fight for it in every field
of life. That is necessary because the idea of liberty isn't really a product
that can be provided either by private enterprise or, of course, its enemy the
state. It must be provided as a gift to civilization.

These are points taught to me by the life and work of Burton Samuel
Blumert, one of liberty's great benefactors. He died at age 80 on the morning of March 30, 2009, after a long battle with cancer. He would deny it,
but his name deserves to go down in history as a person who served as a
champion of freedom during his long life.

He was born in Brooklyn, and after attending NYU and NYU Law
School, and being forced into the Air Force (where the socialist regimentation made him a libertarian), Burt was a fundraiser for the American
Jewish Committee and a store detective for a large retail establishment in
NYC, searching out thieves. Then he was offered a promotion, and also
the chance to be a traveling manager of a chain of ladies hat shops mostly
based in the South, which he loved. However, the firm had a couple of
stores in Northern California, and its first one at Hillsdale Mall, and Burt
fell in love with the area.

---

*March 30, 2009

Luckily, just at the time that "the evil JFK killed the hat," as he put it, Burt had the chance to buy into a business that was also his hobby, Camino Coin in Burlingame. Over the next decades, Burt built Camino into one of the most important dealers on the West Coast. Indeed, the firm became internationally known for its prices and service.

Burt was also a Silicon Valley pioneer, joining all the coins dealers in the country in their first computer network for prices and news. Xerox eventually bought the network. During all this, his libertarianism was not neglected, however, nor his opposition to inflationary fiat money and the Federal Reserve. He helped sponsor speaking engagements for such Austrian economists as Ludwig von Mises and Leonard E. Read, and became a friend and benefactor of many libertarian scholars and activists, especially Murray N. Rothbard.

He served faithfully as chairman of the Mises Institute, succeeding Margit von Mises in that post. He was a dear friend of Murray's, and stuck steadfastly by him when others bailed out on grounds that Murray was too radical or too independent as an intellectual. Blumert saw that this genius needed support, and he provided it in every way. Indeed, in the darkest days, he made the difference.

Rothbard was only one of many who benefited from his generosity and care. Burt never wavered in his support, through thick and thin, providing excellent counsel and guidance at every step. I know that I had come to depend on his unfailing friendship and judgment in a host of areas.

His support was more than financial; he also offered his time and energy with great generosity. He provided offices, the safekeeping of books, and personal encouragement to many libertarian scholars; he linked up scholars with benefactors and publishers and employers, and even drove people to events big and small. And he played an important role as proprietor of Camino, in turning customers into benefactors of libertarian and Austrian organizations.

He had a quiet way about him that was always utterly and completely sincere. It was this feature of Burt that made him a good "salesman," and he was legendary in that respect. He loved helping people achieve financial independence. But it was about more than just business to him. He had the vision to see that ideas are more important than all the world's goods. It was this that he sought to give to the world. His gifts for friendship and hospitality were also essential.

For many years, he served as master of ceremonies for Mises Institute events. He was extremely comfortable, and successful, in asking for people's support of this cause, because he was also a supporter himself. In 2003 he was awarded the first Murray N. Rothbard Prize in celebration of his amazing contribution in a host of areas. He believed he didn't deserve it, of course. But we all sensed that Murray cheered as he accepted it: Attaboy, Burt, he often said.

Many people commented on Burt's sense of humor. It was pervasive, and unfailing in good times and bad. Have a look at his wonderful collection of observations in his book *Bagels, Barry Bonds, and Rotten Politicians*. He used humor as a way of cutting through the ideological thicket created by the political moment, as a means to help people see and understand what truly matters.

It was something that many of us counted on for years. The news would be filled with reports of ominous events and threats to life and property. But Burt had a way of maintaining a refreshing distance, remembering what is important, and bringing humor to lighten the moment so that others could discern what really matters.

His political outlook was decidedly Rothbardian. He saw politicians as predictable in their scammery and racketeering. He saw the state as no more than a massive drain on society, something we could do well without. War he regarded as a massive and destructive diversion of social resources. Welfare he saw as a perverse system for rewarding bad behavior and punishing virtue. Regulations on business he saw as interventions that benefitted the well-connected at the expense of the true heroes of society, who were pursuing enterprise with an eye to independence and profitability.

His main enemy was the inflationary state, and one reason he got into the business of precious metals was to battle paper money. As a lifetime observer of the business cycle, he knew that paper-money and artificial-credit creation lead to illusions that would eventually dissipate. So it was no surprise that he saw the latest bust coming early on. As a resident of the Bay Area in Northern California, he was surrounded by illusions, but his knowledge of Austrian business-cycle theory permitted him to see through the fog.

There was a wonderful realism about his way of looking at society. He hated the state for its sheer phoniness. The paper dollar was just the beginning of it all, the most obvious symbol. To Burt, all of the state's glorious activities were an illusion, creating false booms with every action. It was the sheer hypocrisy of statecraft that struck him the most.

Private markets too have their share of crooks, but at least they didn't sail under the cover of legal legitimacy. Here is what he wrote about his favorite sport, boxing:

> There is a refreshing quality about the world of boxing and the commissions that govern it: corruption is pure and unadulterated. The road to ascendancy in the world of boxing has no moral detours. For those who rise to the top, a stretch at Sing Sing is more valued than an Ivy League degree (and the alumni connections more useful). A murder indictment is equivalent to a graduate degree (see the bio of impresario Don King). There is no waste of resources in locating members for the athletic commission. The marketplace assigns a dollar value on each appointment and the only concern is that the bills are unmarked.

Burt was a wonderful friend to have, a man of extraordinary generosity and sound judgment. He was a living saint to libertarian intellectuals and a dear friend to the remnant that loves freedom. He was self-effacing to the extreme, always sincerely and quickly giving credit to others and refusing it himself. He was also a cook and host of great ability and generosity, and his home was a salon of liberty.

A longtime friend and supporter of Ron Paul, Burt chaired his 1988 Libertarian Party campaign for president, and cheered and supported his 2008 run. Burt was also the founding publisher of LewRockwell.com, and an important writer for it.

So in his death, let us say what is true about him, simply because he would never let anyone say it about him in life. Through his daily life and good works, his loyalty and indefatigability, he showed us a path forward, the very model of how a successful businessman can achieve greatness in a lifetime. His legacy can be found in many of the books you read and in the massive growth of libertarianism in our times. Signs of his works are all around us. These were his gifts to the world. And for those of us who knew him, Burt's wonderful life and outlook are gifts to us of inestimable value.

We will miss him every day, but no day will ever pass when we are not inspired by his example. May his great soul rest in peace.

CHAPTER 16

Ron Paul and the Future*

O ne of the most thrilling memories of the 2012 campaign was the sight of those huge crowds who came out to see Ron. His competitors, meanwhile, couldn't fill half a Starbucks. When I worked as Ron's chief of staff in the late 1970s and early 1980s, I could only dream of such a day.

Now what was it that attracted all these people to Ron Paul? He didn't offer his followers a spot on the federal gravy train. He didn't pass some phony bill. In fact, he didn't do any of the things we associate with politicians. What his supporters love about him has nothing to do with politics at all.

Ron is the anti-politician. He tells unfashionable truths, educates rather than flatters the public, and stands up for principle even when the whole world is arrayed against him.

Some people say, "I love Ron Paul, except for his foreign policy." But that foreign policy reflects the best and most heroic part of who Ron Paul is. Peace is the linchpin of the Paulian program, not an extraneous or dispensable adjunct to it. He would never and could never abandon it.

Here was the issue Ron could have avoided had he cared only for personal advancement.

*August 25, 2012

But he refused. No matter how many times he's been urged to keep his mouth shut about war and empire, these have remained the centerpieces of his speeches and interviews.

Of course, Ron Paul deserves the Nobel Peace Prize. In a just world, he would also win the Medal of Freedom, and all the honors for which a man in his position is eligible.

But history is littered with forgotten politicians who earned piles of awards handed out by other politicians. What matters to Ron more than all the honors and ceremonies in the world is all of you, and your commitment to the immortal ideas he has championed all his life.

It's Ron's truth-telling and his urge to educate the public that should inspire us as we carry on into the future.

It isn't a coincidence that governments everywhere want to educate children. Government education, in turn, is supposed to be evidence of the state's goodness and its concern for our well-being. The real explanation is less flattering. If the government's propaganda can take root as children grow up, those kids will be no threat to the state apparatus. They'll fasten the chains to their own ankles.

H.L. Mencken once said that the state doesn't just want to make you obey. It tries to make you *want* to obey. And that's one thing the government schools do very well.

A long-forgotten political thinker, Etienne de la Boétie, wondered why people would ever tolerate an oppressive regime. After all, the people who are governed vastly outnumber the small minority doing the governing. So the people governed could put a stop to it all if only they had the will to do so. And yet they rarely do.

De la Boétie concluded that the only way any regime could survive was if the public consented to it. That consent could range all the way from enthusiastic support to stoic resignation. But if that consent were ever to vanish, a regime's days would be numbered.

And that's why education—real education—is such a threat to any regime. If the state loses its grip over your mind, it loses the key to its very survival.

The state is beginning to lose that grip. Traditional media, which have carried water for the government since time began, it seems, are threatened by independent voices on the Internet. I don't think anyone under 25 even reads a newspaper.

The media and the political class joined forces to try to make sure you never found out about Ron Paul. When that proved impossible, they smeared him, and told you no one could want to go hear Ron when they could hear Tim Pawlenty or Mitt Romney instead.

All this backfired. The more they panicked about Ron, the more drawn to him people were. They wanted to know what it was that the Establishment was so eager to keep them from hearing.

Ours is the most radical challenge to the state ever posed. We aren't trying to make the state more efficient, or show how it can take in more revenue, or change its pattern of wealth redistribution. We're not saying that this subsidy is better than that one, or that this kind of tax would make the system run more smoothly than that one. We reject the existing system root and branch.

And we don't oppose the state's wars because they'll be counterproductive or overextend the state's forces. We oppose them because mass murder based on lies can never be morally acceptable.

So we don't beg for scraps from the imperial table, and we don't seek a seat at that table. We want to knock the table over.

We have much work to do. Countless Americans have been persuaded that it's in their interest to be looted and ordered around by a ruling elite that in fact cares nothing for their welfare and seeks only to increase its power and wealth at their expense.

The most lethal and anti-social institution in history has gotten away with describing itself as the very source of civilization. From the moment they set foot in the government's schools, Americans learn that the state is there to rescue them from poverty, unsafe medicines, and rainy days, to provide economic stimulus when the economy is poor, and to keep them secure against shadowy figures everywhere. This view is reinforced, in turn, by the broadcast and print media.

If the public has been bamboozled, as Murray Rothbard would say, it is up to us to do the de-bamboozling. We need to tear the benign mask off the state.

That is the task before you, before all of us, here today.

Begin with yourself. Learn everything you can about a free society. Read the greats, like Frédéric Bastiat, Ludwig von Mises, and Murray Rothbard. As you delve into the literature of liberty, share what you're reading and learning. Start a blog. Create a YouTube channel. Organize a reading group. But whatever you do, learn, spread what you're learning, and never stop.

If it is through propaganda that people thoughtlessly accept the claims of the state, then it is through education that people must be brought to their senses.

With its kept media on the wane, it is going to be more and more difficult for the state to make its claims stick, to persuade people to keep accepting its lies and propaganda.

You've heard it said that the pen is mightier than the sword. Think of the sword as the state. Think of the pen as all of you, each in your own way, spreading the ideas of liberty.

Remember that insight of Etienne de la Boétie: all government rests on public consent, and as soon as the public withdraws that consent, any regime is doomed.

This is why they fear Ron, it's why they fear you, and it's why, despite the horrors we read about every day, we may dare to look to the future with hope.

CHAPTER 17

The Generosity
of Murray Rothbard*

I t is a magnificent thing that Murray Rothbard's most overlooked masterpiece, his *Austrian Perspective on the History of Economic Thought*,
has now been made available free online in two volumes, with complete
navigation tools: *Economic Thought Before Adam Smith* and *Classical
Economics*.

It is the culmination of a process that began in the 1980s with the original research and writing, and many lectures, often presented at the offices
of the Mises Institute. Finally, these volumes appeared in print in 1995, the
year he died. But they were so expensive that they were unaffordable for
regular people. In 2006, the Mises Institute was able to publish both volumes at a fraction of the original price. Now, at last, the ideas have been set
free with complete online editions.

There are not enough superlatives to describe what Rothbard has done
in these books. He was not of the view that progress always defines the
trajectory of ideas over time. He looked for truth in the ancient world, the
middle ages, and modern times, while spotting error and outright evil in
all times as well. He is fearless in naming names. The result is a remarkable
intellectual drama, one so compelling that it will redefine the way you look
at the course of history itself.

---

*March 24, 2009

It is not just the astonishing level of research, but the ebullient energy of Rothbard's personality and prose. Open any page and see what happens. Looking randomly now at page 33 in volume one, we get a round up of the early Christian fathers and theologians. Tertullian was hostile to the merchant class partly because he expected the world to founder at any moment on the shoals of excess population. St. Jerome was not much better: he extolled the zero-sum view of wealth: "the rich man is unjust, or the heir of an unjust one."

The best of the lot was Clement of Alexandria, who celebrated private property and warned,

> We must not cast away riches which can benefit our neighbor. Possessions were made to be possessed; goods are called goods because they do good, and they have been provided by God for the good of men: they are at hand and serve as the material, the instruments for a good use in the hand of him who knows how to use them.

Fascinating, isn't it? That's about one one-millionth of what you get here. To read these books is like finding yourself at the most opulent banquet you can imagine, with an endless variety of foods prepared by the world's greatest chefs, and everything is free. But there is a difference between culinary satisfaction and this intellectual feast. The mind is capable of far more consumption than the body, and Rothbard lavishes us with ideas. You get the sense that he just can't wait to tell you what he has discovered. He has your attention and is thrilled, and hopes to engage you for as long as possible on the topic at hand. He draws you into this world and ends up making what some might think is a boring topic come alive and just about take over your life.

It's a wonderful work, and it tells you something about the person that he was. His number-one passion was research and his number-two passion was telling others about what he had found. In this sense, he was remarkably self-effacing. After all, he was an innovator like few minds in human history. His unique contributions to economic theory comprise a long list. More than that, he was the first to fully integrate economic science, moral philosophy, and political theory in a unified theory of liberty. To say that is not an exaggeration in the slightest. He was the founder of modern libertarianism, a theory of politics that is so compelling that once you have absorbed it, it becomes the lens through which you end up understanding all economic and political events. The best roundup of the whole of Rothbardian thought, by the way, is this excellent small book by David Gordon: *The Essential Rothbard.*

Oddly, however, Rothbard himself doesn't figure into his own history of ideas. It's not just that he never got around to writing about the 20th century. There is more at work. What we see here is a fascinating combination of generosity and humility, a man far more interested in promoting the sound ideas of others rather than his own work.

We saw this in the course of his life, and once we understand it, we gain insight into the unusual personal conflicts that have been fodder for gossip and legend in libertarian circles for decades. Justin Raimondo does a fine job of discussing many of these in his biography *Enemy of the State.* He shows that the history of personality conflicts that peppered the life of Rothbard really amount to a long series of personal betrayals of a benefactor (the worst sin, in Dante's view).

And yet this raises the question: why were there so many who benefited from Rothbard's personal mentorship and later turned on him to denounce him and try so hard to topple him from his position as Mr. Libertarian? Some, like the billionaire Charles Koch, attempted to run his name out of public life, as documented in Brian Doherty's *Radicals for Capitalism.*

Here is a stab at a reason. To be around Rothbard, and to be part of his circle of friends, was an enormously flattering experience. He made everyone feel brilliant and important. He wasn't the sort to insist that one sit at his feet and learn from him. He drew you in and made you feel as if you were making a great contribution to a historic project. If you made a point that he thought was a good one, he would praise you to the skies.

If you go through Rothbard's work, you find an unleashed passion for giving others credit for contributions to the history of ideas. His *Ethics of Liberty*, for example, is replete with citations to people who otherwise made no mark. The people who entered into his world began to think of themselves as Rothbard's intellectual equals, and this was not an accident. It was something that Rothbard himself encouraged. He was radically against the creation of a personality cult, and instead shared and spread his ideas with profligate abandon.

These people came to be so flattered by his attention, and so absorbed into his approach, that they actually started to believe that Rothbard himself was dispensable. There was usually some precipitating event. The Rothbardian would write an article that departed from the master in some respect. Rothbard might have said nothing, but this was not his way. He longed for intellectual engagement, so he would come back and engage, usually in a way that harmed the pride of the disciple. The disciple would take it all personally and turn on the master in a life-changing way, and swear eternal enmity. This happened time and again, even for some not in the Koch ambit.

But consider the driving force here. Rothbard was so generous, so flattering to those around him, that his disciples felt empowered to the point that they actually believed that they were on Rothbard's intellectual level and could easily break off on their own and become famous. A telling fact, however, is that none of these people—and there were many—really did anything on their own, and what they did do amounted to recycling what Rothbard had taught them without giving him credit. That's a short history of how it came to be that Rothbard, one of the century's brightest lights, rarely received the credit he deserved during his lifetime.

Now, nearly fifteen years after his death, his star is higher than ever, with a new edition of *Man, Economy, and State* just published, and his triumphant *History of Economic Thought* now online for the whole world.

He continues to teach us all, as generous as he was in life. Fortunately, now he is also getting the credit, while even his detractors can only stand in awe at his current influence.

CHAPTER 18

Twin Demons*

The 20th century was the century of total war. Limitations on the scope of war, built up over many centuries, had already begun to break down in the 19th century, but they were altogether obliterated in the 20th. And of course the sheer amount of resources that centralized states could bring to bear in war, and the terrible new technologies of killing that became available to them, made the 20th a century of almost unimaginable horror.

It isn't terribly often that people discuss the development of total war in tandem with the development of modern central banking, which—although antecedents existed long before—also came into its own in the 20th century. It's no surprise that Ron Paul, the man in public life who has done more than anyone to break through the limits of what is permissible to say in polite society about both these things, has also been so insistent that the twin phenomena of war and central banking are linked. "It is no coincidence," Dr. Paul said, "that the century of total war coincided with the century of central banking."

He added:

> If every American taxpayer had to submit an extra five or ten thousand dollars to the IRS this April to pay for the war, I'm

---

*September 26, 2012

quite certain it would end very quickly. The problem is that government finances war by borrowing and printing money, rather than presenting a bill directly in the form of higher taxes. When the costs are obscured, the question of whether any war is worth it becomes distorted.

For the sake of my remarks today I take it as given that Murray Rothbard's analysis of the true functions of central banking is correct. Rothbard's books *The History of Money and Banking: The Colonial Era Through World War II, The Case Against the Fed, The Mystery of Banking,* and *What Has Government Done to Our Money?* provide the logical case and the empirical evidence for this view, and I refer you to those sources for additional details.

For now I take it as uncontroversial that central banks perform three significant functions for the banking system and the government. First, they serve as lenders of last resort, which in practice means bailouts for the big financial firms. Second, they coordinate the inflation of the money supply by establishing a uniform rate at which the banks inflate, thereby making the fractional-reserve banking system less unstable and more consistently profitable than it would be without a central bank (which, by the way, is why the banks themselves always clamor for a central bank). Finally, they allow governments, via inflation, to finance their operations far more cheaply and surreptitiously than they otherwise could.

As an enabler of inflation, the Fed is ipso facto an enabler of war. Looking back on World War I, Ludwig von Mises wrote in 1919, "One can say without exaggeration that inflation is an indispensable means of militarism. Without it, the repercussions of war on welfare become obvious much more quickly and penetratingly; war weariness would set in much earlier."

No government has ever said, "Because we want to go to war, we must abandon central banking," or "Because we want to go to war, we must abandon inflation and the fiat money system." Governments always say, "We must abandon the gold standard because we want to go to war." That alone indicates the restraint that hard money places on governments. Precious metals cannot be created out of thin air, which is why governments chafe at monetary systems based on them.

Governments can raise revenue in three ways. Taxation is the most visible means of doing so, and it eventually meets with popular resistance. They can borrow the money they need, but this borrowing is likewise visible to the public in the form of higher interest rates—as the federal government competes for a limited amount of available credit, credit becomes scarcer for other borrowers.

Creating money out of thin air, the third option, is preferable for governments, since the process by which the political class siphons resources from society via inflation is far less direct and obvious than in the cases of taxation and borrowing. In the old days the kings clipped the coins, kept the shavings, then spent the coins back into circulation with the same nominal value. Once they have it, governments guard this power jealously. Mises once said that if the Bank of England had been available to King Charles I during the English Civil War of the 1640s, he could have crushed the parliamentary forces arrayed against him, and English history would have been much different.

Juan de Mariana, a Spanish Jesuit who wrote in the 16th and early 17th centuries, is best known in political philosophy for having defended regicide in his 1599 work *De Rege*. Casual students often assume that it must have been for this provocative claim that the Spanish government confined him for a time. But in fact it was his *Treatise on the Alteration of Money*, which condemned monetary inflation as a moral evil, that got him in trouble.

Think about that. Saying the king could be killed was one thing. But taking direct aim at inflation, the lifeblood of the regime? Now that was taking things too far.

In those days, if a war were to be funded partly by monetary debasement, the process was direct and not difficult to understand. The sequence of events today is more complicated, but as I've said, not fundamentally different. What happens today is not that the government needs to pay for a war, comes up short, and simply prints the money to make up the difference. The process is not quite so crude. But when we examine it carefully, it turns out to be essentially the same thing.

Central banks, established by the world's governments, allow those governments to spend more than they receive in taxes. Borrowing allowed them to spend more than they received in taxes, but government borrowing led to higher interest rates, which in turn can provoke the public in undesirable ways. When central banks create money and inject it into the banking system, they serve the purposes of governments by pushing those interest rates back down, thereby concealing the effects of government borrowing.

But central banking does more than this. It essentially prints up money and hands it to the government, though not quite so directly and obviously.

First, the federal government is able to sell its bonds at artificially high prices (and correspondingly low interest rates) because the buyers of its debt know they can turn around and sell to the Federal Reserve. It's true that the federal government has to pay interest on the securities the Federal Reserve owns, but at the end of the year the Fed pays that money back to the Treasury, minus its trivial operating expenses. That takes care of the interest. And in case you're thinking that the federal government still has to pay out at least the principal, it really doesn't. The government can roll over its existing debt when it comes due, issuing a new bond to pay off the principal of the old one.

Through this convoluted process—a process, not coincidentally, that the general public is unlikely to know about or understand—the federal government is in fact able to do the equivalent of printing money and spending it. While everyone else has to acquire resources by spending money they earned in a productive enterprise—in other words, they first have to produce something for society, and then they may consume—government may acquire resources without first having produced anything. Money creation via government monopoly thus becomes another mechanism whereby the exploitative relationship between government and the public is perpetuated.

Now because the central bank allows the government to conceal the cost of everything it does, it provides an incentive for governments to engage in additional spending in all kinds of areas, not just war. But because war is enormously expensive and because the sacrifices that accompany it place such a strain on the public, it is wartime expenditures for which the assistance of the central bank is especially welcome for any government.

The Federal Reserve System, which was established in late 1913 and opened its doors the following year, was first put to the test during World War I. Unlike some countries, the United States did not abandon the gold standard during the war, but it was not operating under a pure 100 percent gold standard in any case. The Fed could and did engage in credit expansion. On Mises.org we feature an article by John Paul Koning that takes the reader through the exact process by which the Fed carried out its monetary inflation in those early years. In brief, the Fed essentially created money and used it to add war bonds to its balance sheet. Benjamin Anderson, the Austrian-sympathetic economist, observed at the time, "The growth in virtually all the items of the balance sheet of the Federal Reserve System since the United States entered the war has been very great indeed."

The Fed's accommodating role was not confined to wartime itself. In *America's Money Machine*, Elgin Groseclose wrote,

> Although the war was over in 1918, in a fighting sense, it was not over in a financial sense. The Treasury still had enormous obligations to meet, which were eventually covered by a Victory loan. The main support in the market again was the Federal Reserve.

Monetary expansion was especially helpful to the US government during the Vietnam War. Lyndon Johnson could have both his Great Society programs and his overseas war, and the strain on the public was kept—at first, at least—within manageable limits.

So confident had the Keynesian economic planners become that by 1970, Arthur Okun, one of the decade's key presidential advisers on the economy, was noting in a published retrospective that wise economic management seemed to have done away with the business cycle. But reality could not be evaded forever, and the apparently strong war economy of the 1960s gave way to the stagnation of the 1970s.

There is a law of the universe according to which every time the public is promised that the boom-bust business cycle has been banished forever, a bust is right around the corner. One month after Okun's rosy book was published, the recession began.

Americans paid a steep cost for the inflation of the 1960s. The loss of life resulting from the war itself was the most gruesome and horrific of these costs, but the economic devastation cannot be ignored. As many of us well remember, years of unemployment and high inflation plagued the US economy. The stock market fared even worse. Mark Thornton points out that

> in May 1970, a portfolio consisting of one share of every stock listed on the Big Board was worth just about half of what it would have been worth at the start of 1969. The high flyers that had led the market of 1967 and 1968—conglomerates, computer leasers, far-out electronics companies, franchisers—were precipitously down from their peaks. Nor were they down 25 percent, like the Dow, but 80, 90, or 95 percent.
>
> … The Dow index shows that stocks tended to trade in a wide channel for much of the period between 1965 and 1984. However, if you adjust the value of stocks by price inflation as measured by the Consumer Price Index, a clearer and more disturbing picture emerges. The inflation-adjusted or real purchasing

power measure of the Dow indicates that it lost nearly 80% of its peak value.

And for all the talk of the Fed's alleged independence, it is not even possible to imagine the Fed maintaining a tight-money stance when the regime demands stimulus, or when the troops are in the field. It has been more than accommodating during the so-called War on Terror. Consider the amount of debt purchased every year by the Fed, and compare it to that year's war expenditures, and you will get a sense of the Fed's enabling role.

Now while it's true that a gold standard restrains governments, it's also true that governments have little difficulty finding pretexts—war chief among them—to abandon the gold standard. For that reason, the gold standard in and of itself is not a sufficient restraint on the government's ambitions, at home and abroad.

As we look to the future, we must cast aside all timidity in our proposals for monetary reform. We do not seek a gold-exchange standard, as existed under the Bretton Woods system. We do not seek to use the price of gold as a calibration device to assist the monetary authority in its decisions on how much money to create. We do not even seek the restoration of the classical gold standard, great though its merits are.

In the 1830s, the hard-money Jacksonian monetary theorists coined the marvelous phrase "separation of bank and state." That would be a start.

What we need today is the separation of money and state.

There are some ways in which money is unique among goods. For one thing, money is valued not for its own sake but for its use in exchange. For another, money is not consumed, but rather is handed on from one person to another. And all other goods in the economy have their prices expressed in terms of this good.

But there is nothing about money—or anything else, for that matter—that should make us think its production must be carried out by the government or its designated monopoly grantee. Money constitutes one-half of every non-barter market transaction. People who believe in the market economy, and yet who are prepared to hand over to the state the custodianship of this most crucial good, ought to think again.

Interventionists sometimes claim that a particular good is just too important to be left to the market. The standard free-market reply turns this argument around: the more important a commodity is, the more essential it is for the government not to produce it, and to leave its production to the market instead.

Nowhere is this more true than in the case of money. As Ludwig von Mises once said, the history of money is the history of government efforts to destroy money. Government control of money has yielded monetary debasement, the impoverishment of society relative to the state, devastating business cycles, financial bubbles, capital consumption (because of falsified profit-and-loss accounting), moral hazard, and—most germane to my topic today—the expropriation of the public in ways they are unlikely to understand. It is this silent expropriation that has made possible some of the state's greatest enormities, including its wars, and it is all of these offenses combined that constitute a compelling popular brief against the current system and in favor of a market substitute.

The war machine and the money machine, in short, are intimately linked. It is vain to denounce the moral grotesqueries of the US empire without at the same time taking aim at the indispensable support that makes it all possible. If we wish to oppose the state and all its manifestations—its imperial adventures, its domestic subsidies, its unstoppable spending and debt accumulation—we must point to their source, the central bank, the mechanism that the state and its kept media and economists will defend to their dying days.

The state has persuaded the people that its own interests are identical with theirs. It seeks to promote their welfare. Its wars are their wars. It is the great benefactor, and the people are to be content in their role as its contented subjects.

Ours is a different view. The state's relationship to the people is not benign, it is not one of magnanimous giver and grateful recipient. It is an exploitative relationship, whereby an array of self-perpetuating fiefdoms that produce nothing live at the expense of the toiling majority. Its wars do not protect the public; they fleece it. Its subsidies do not promote the so-called public good; they undermine it. Why should we expect its production of money to be an exception to this general pattern?

As F.A. Hayek said, it is not reasonable to think that the state has any interest in giving us a "good money." What the state wants is to produce the money or have a privileged position vis-à-vis the source of the money, so it can dispense largesse to its favored constituencies. We should not be anxious to accommodate it.

The state does not compromise, and neither should we. In the struggle of liberty against power, few enough will oppose the state and the conventional wisdom it urges us to adopt. Fewer still will reject the state and its programs root and branch. We must be those few, as we work toward a future in which we are the many.

This is our mission today, as it has been the mission of the Mises Institute for the past 30 years. With your support, we shall at this critical moment carry on publishing our books and periodicals, aiding research and teaching in Austrian economics, promoting the Austrian School to the public, and training tomorrow's champions of the economics of freedom.

CHAPTER 19

Emulate Ron Paul*

I've had the privilege of knowing Ron Paul for 37 years. I worked as his chief of staff during his early years in Congress, and he played an important role when I opened the Mises Institute, where he has served as our distinguished counselor ever since.

He's the same person in private life that he is in public: thoughtful, decent, humble, self-effacing, and generous in acknowledging his intellectual debts.

These are not qualities people associate with political figures. That's part of the reason Ron became such a phenomenon.

More than anything else, Ron has been a teacher throughout his years in public life. In his articles and speeches, and even in the bills he introduced, he sought to convey the philosophy of liberty and what that philosophy implies for our daily lives. His books, which include numerous bestsellers, have done the same thing. Compare Ron's books to Mitt Romney's, and you'll see what I mean.

But as the person who reached more people with the message of liberty than anyone in our time, Ron has also taught us how that message can and must be spread. I want to talk about five of these lessons tonight.

---

*April 6, 2013

#1 THE SUBJECT OF WAR CANNOT, AND SHOULD NOT, BE AVOIDED.

First and foremost, Ron is a critic of the warfare state.

The war in Iraq, which was still a live issue when Ron first ran for the Republican nomination, had been sold to the public on the basis of lies that were transparent and insulting even by the US government's standards. The devastation—in terms of deaths, maimings, displacement, and sheer destruction—appalled every decent human being.

Yes, the Department of Education is an outrage, but it is nothing next to the horrifying images of what happened to the men, women, and children of Iraq. If he wasn't going to denounce such a clear moral evil, Ron thought, what was the point of being in public life at all?

Still, this is the issue strategists would have had him avoid. Just talk about the budget, talk about the greatness of America, talk about whatever everyone else was talking about, and you'll be fine. And, they neglected to add, forgotten.

But had Ron shied away from this issue, there would have been no Ron Paul Revolution. It was his courageous refusal to back down from certain unspeakable truths about the American role in the world that caused Americans, and especially students, to sit up and take notice.

While still in his thirties, Murray Rothbard wrote privately that he was beginning to view war as "*the* key to the whole libertarian business." Here is another way Ron Paul has been faithful to the Rothbardian tradition. Time after time, in interviews and public appearances, Ron has brought the questions posed to him back to the central issues of war and foreign policy.

Worried about the budget? You can't run an empire on the cheap. Concerned about TSA groping, or government eavesdropping, or cameras trained on you? These are the inevitable policies of a hegemon. In case after case, Ron pointed to the connection between an imperial policy abroad and abuses and outrages at home.

Inspired by Ron, libertarians began to challenge conservatives by reminding them that war, after all, is the ultimate government program. War has it all: propaganda, censorship, spying, crony contracts, money printing, skyrocketing spending, debt creation, central planning, hubris—everything we associate with the worst interventions into the economy.

Robert Higgs, in his classic book *Crisis and Leviathan*, showed how war left longstanding scars on American society, as power and wealth grabbed by the federal government during wartime were never relinquished in their entirety when hostilities ended. When Franklin Roosevelt launched his

New Deal in the 1930s, he appealed to ideological and statutory precedents established during the American involvement in World War I.

But Ron Paul permanently changed the nature of the discussion on war and foreign policy. The word "nonintervention" rarely appeared in foreign-policy discussions before 2007. Opposition to war was associated with anti-capitalist causes. That is no longer the case.

Ron kept insisting that there was no real foreign policy debate in America because all we were allowed to do was argue over what kind of intervention the US government should pursue. Whether intervention itself was desirable, or whether the bipartisan assumptions behind US foreign policy were sound—this was not even mentioned, much less debated.

In exposing the fraudulent American foreign policy debate, Ron exposed an overlooked truth about American political life. The debates Americans are allowed to have are ones in which the real decisions have already been made: income tax or consumption tax, fiscal stimulus or monetary stimulus, sanctions or war, later war or war right away. With debates like these, it hardly matters who wins. Ron pulled back the curtain on all of it.

#2 TELL THE TRUTH.

It wasn't just on war that Ron defied the censors of opinion. Ask Ron Paul a question, and you get an answer. In Miami he said the embargo on Cuba needed to be lifted. In South Carolina he stuck to his guns on the drug war. He never ran away from a question, or twisted it, in spin-doctor fashion, into the question he wished he had been asked.

And the audiences kept growing: thousands and thousands of students were coming out to see him, at a time when his competitors could barely fill half a bingo hall.

Ron knew that the philosophy of liberty, when explained persuasively and with conviction, had a universal appeal. Every group he spoke to heard a slightly different presentation of that message, as Ron showed how their particular concerns were addressed most effectively by a policy of freedom.

When Ron first spoke to the so-called values voters, for example, he was booed for saying he worshipped the Prince of Peace. The second time, when he again made a moral case for freedom, he brought the house down. But he did not pander to them nor to anyone else, and he never abandoned the philosophy that brought him into public life in the first place. No one had the sense that there was more than one Ron Paul, that he was trying to satisfy irreconcilable groups. There was one Ron Paul.

#3 THE PROBLEM IS NOT ONE PERSON, NOR ONE PARTY.

Michelle Malkin writes books about the corruption in Democratic administrations. The same books could be written about Republican administrations, and indeed they sometimes are, by the partisans of the other side. Meanwhile, Americans are tricked into thinking that we just need to root out a few bad apples, or that the problems we face are caused by this or that group of occupants of the seats of power.

Ron rarely gets worked up about some government functionary who had been receiving some graft. Yes, this is wrong, and yes, the guy should be sacked.

But to spend inordinate time on the scandal of the day is to suggest that if only we had good people in charge, the system would work. The vast bulk of what the state does shouldn't be done at all, with good *or* bad people, and whatever else it does can be far better managed by free individuals.

If a government official spends inordinate sums on vacations and luxuries, or is exposed for being on the take, be assured that the person's political opponents will be all over the story. Meanwhile, the inherent corruption of the system itself, with its systematic expropriation and redistribution, is ignored. But that is by far the more important story, and it's the only one that really deserves our attention.

#4 THERE IS MORE TO LIFE, AND MORE TO LIBERTY, THAN POLITICS.

Before leaving Washington and electoral politics, Ron delivered an extraordinary farewell address to Congress. The very fact that Ron could deliver a wise and learned address only goes to show he was no run-of-the-mill congressman, whose intellectual life is fulfilled by talking points and focus-group results.

That a farewell address seemed so appropriate for Ron in the first place, while it would have been risible for virtually any of his colleagues, reflected Ron's substance and seriousness as a thinker and as a man.

In that address Ron did many things. He surveyed his many years in Congress. He made a reckoning of the advance of the state and the retreat of liberty. He explained the moral ideas at the root of the libertarian message: nonaggression and freedom. He posed a series of questions about the US government and American society that are hardly ever asked, much less answered. And he gave his supporters advice on spreading the message in the coming years.

"Achieving legislative power and political influence," he said, should not be our goal. Most of the change, if it is to come, will not come from the politicians, but rather from individuals, family, friends, intellectual leaders, and our religious institutions. The solution can only come from rejecting the use of coercion, compulsion, government commands, and aggressive force, to mold social and economic behavior.

How many bills did Ron Paul get passed, his neoconservative opponents demand to know. I think of it this way. No one is going to remember any bill that Rick Santorum's advisers drafted for him. No one is going to remember Rick Santorum. Ron Paul, on the other hand, will be remembered. Of how many other congressmen can it be said that they (1) urged students to read thousand-page treatises on economics, and (2) the students actually did it?

Today, at a major homeschool convention in Ohio, Ron announced the Ron Paul Homeschool Curriculum. His program covers Kindergarten through 12th grade. Students will be exposed to thinkers they would never encounter in a government school. They will know history and economics better than anyone their age.

They will learn public speaking, and writing, and social media. They will emerge as top-notch ambassadors of the ideas Ron has championed his whole life. They will, I predict, join Young Americans for Liberty.

There is no bill that Newt Gingrich, or Rick Santorum, or the rest of them ever got passed that amounts to a grain of sand compared to what Ron Paul will accomplish in just this one endeavor, by educating young students.

#5 THE FED CANNOT BE IGNORED.

No focus groups urged Ron to talk about the Federal Reserve. No politician had made an issue of the Fed in an election in its 100-year history. Stick to the script, the professionals would have said: lower taxes and lower spending, the monotonous refrain uttered by every Republican politician, who typically has no interest in carrying through with either one anyway.

Yet Ron pointed to the Fed as the source of the boom-bust cycle that has harmed so many Americans. His dogged insistence on this point got a great many Americans curious: what, after all, was the Fed, and what was it up to? An unlikely issue, to be sure, and yet it was his willingness to talk about it that in my view helps to account for much of his fundraising success. There was a small but untapped portion of the public that responded with enthusiasm to Ron's very mention of the Fed, and they wanted more.

Here again, had Ron adopted conventional political advice, he would have forfeited these historic moments and the Ron Paul phenomenon would have been greatly diminished, if not compromised altogether.

Only a few months after Ron officially suspended his 2008 campaign, the financial crisis struck. Just as Ron had said, there was something indeed wrong with the economy. His opponents, meanwhile, were exposed as the fools and charlatans we knew them to be. Just one week before that crisis hit, Herman Cain was dismissing all complaints and warnings about the economy as nothing but an anti-Republican media conspiracy.

John McCain, meanwhile, the party's nominee, had said the fundamentals of the economy were sound, and that although he wasn't an expert on the economy, he was reading Alan Greenspan's book.

Because he hadn't hesitated to say what he believed, even if it meant dealing with an issue no political operative would have encouraged him to discuss, Ron was a prophet. That point alone opened countless more people to Ron's ideas: here was the only guy in Washington who warned us of what was to come. (And incidentally, has there been a time in American history in which more people were reading—and writing!—anti-Fed books?)

People could see, too, that Ron hadn't just gotten lucky in 2007 and 2008. In 2001, Ron said on the House floor that the Fed-fueled bubble in tech stocks, which had just burst, was being replaced by a Fed-fueled real-estate bubble, which would burst just as surely.

* * * * *

I mentioned earlier that Ron has left politics. To the media, for whom political life is everything, that meant Ron would henceforth be invisible. They wish.

Ron is putting his money where his mouth is: when he says there's more to life than politics, he means it. And he's going to prove it.

I already mentioned his forthcoming homeschool curriculum, which will be enormously influential and do more good than we can imagine.

But he is going to do so much more: in television production, with a new website, in commentary, in speaking, with a new institution on the most important issue, with new books—including a homeschooling manifesto—and much more.

When a well-known radio host asked Ron what he'd be doing in retirement, Ron responded, "Well, they're not putting me in a rocking chair, I can tell you that!"

You can say that again. Ron is stepping everything up.

I am convinced that historians, whether or not they agree with him, will continue to marvel at Ron Paul for many, many years to come. Libertarians a century from now will be in disbelief at the very notion that such a man actually served in the US Congress of our time.

But my purpose tonight has not solely been to pay tribute to Ron, though I am always happy to honor my friend—whose shining example deserves far more than my own words. In reviewing Ron's public life, I've picked out ideas and lessons that must live on.

It is your great task, the young men and women of this organization—which developed out of Students for Ron Paul—who have taken such inspiration from this great man, to embody these ideas and lessons.

For what is Ron's legacy? It is all of you. You reflect what Ron has stood for his whole life. You crave knowledge and understanding. You are not afraid to stand against the establishment—in fact, you relish it. You know the message of liberty will grow not by running away from it, minimizing it, compromising it, or being ashamed of it, but by embracing the great moral ideal it represents.

America and the world are groaning under the burden of war, fiat money, economic crisis, expanding police states, and official lawlessness. It's true that we predicted the outcome we're seeing today, but more importantly, we also know the way out.

If you love and want to spread Ron Paul's message at this critical moment in history, follow his example. It is the only sure path for those who believe in liberty, and who seek its triumph in our lifetimes.

Subject Index

The Mises Institute, founded in 1982, is a teaching and research center for the study of Austrian economics, libertarian and classical liberal political theory, and peaceful international relations. In support of the school of thought represented by Ludwig von Mises, Murray N. Rothbard, Henry Hazlitt, and F.A. Hayek, we publish books and journals, sponsor student and professional conferences, and provide online education. Mises.org is a vast resource of free material for anyone in the world interested in these ideas.

For more information, see Mises.org, write us at info@mises.org, or phone us at 1.800.OF.MISES.

Mises Institute
518 West Magnolia Avenue
Auburn, Alabama 36832

Made in the USA
San Bernardino, CA
27 April 2015